PRINCE HARRY

The Biography

© **Copyright 2022 - All rights reserved.**

The content contained within this book may not be reproduced, duplicated or transmitted without direct written permission from the author or the publisher.

Under no circumstances will any blame or legal responsibility be held against the publisher, or author, for any damages, reparation, or monetary loss due to the information contained within this book, either directly or indirectly.

Legal Notice:

This book is copyright protected. It is only for personal use. You cannot amend, distribute, sell, use, quote or paraphrase any part, or the content within this book, without the consent of the author or publisher.

Disclaimer Notice:

Please note the information contained within this document is for educational and entertainment purposes only. All effort has been executed to present accurate, up to date, reliable, complete information. No warranties of any kind are declared or implied. Readers acknowledge that the author is not engaging in the rendering of legal, financial, medical or professional advice. The content within this book has been derived from various sources. Please consult a licensed professional before attempting any techniques outlined in this book.

By reading this document, the reader agrees that under no circumstances is the author responsible for any losses, direct or indirect, that are incurred as a result of the use of information contained within this document, including, but not limited to, errors, omissions, or inaccuracies.

CONTENTS

Introduction 1

Chapter 1: The Early Years 9

Chapter 2: The Divorce and
Death of Princess Diana 31

Chapter 3: The Heir and the Spare 52

Chapter 4: Meghan Markle 77

Chapter 5: The Crownless Prince 98

Chapter 6: A Royal No More 118

Conclusion 154

References 160

Introduction

Ever since Prince Harry and his wife, Meghan Markle—the Duke and Duchess of Sussex—announced that they were taking a step back from their royal duties, their names became a constant presence in the daily press and social media. Feelings about their actions range anywhere from total support to abject hatred. However, the couple is far from the first members of the British Royal Family whose actions have divided the people of the United Kingdom and the world at large. In fact, controversial decisions are something of a tradition for those close to the British Crown, stemming all the way back to its inception.

In more recent times, public discourse surrounding Harry and Meghan is very reminiscent of the situations involving Harry's parents, King Charles III and the late Princess Diana, and the briefly enthroned King Edward VIII, the paternal uncle of Harry's grandmother, Queen Elizabeth II, and his eventual wife, Wallis Simpson. Many of the problems faced by the Sussexes were also faced by those other two controversial couples, particularly the alternately combative and supportive relationships maintained with the general public and media.

Edward VIII and Wallis Simpson seemed to lay the groundwork for the way that forces outside of the Royal Family could bully its members into taking a certain course of action that isolated the subjects of their ire from the rest of the family. The two biggest concerns vocalized in the press about Edward and Wallis were the fact that she was an American actress rather than part of the British gentry or nobility and that she had two previous marriages and divorces. Divorce had long since been a controversial topic when it came to members of the Royal Family, and many would go to great lengths to avoid it.

King Henry VIII broke with the Roman Catholic Church in the 1500s, establishing the Church of England as an independent religious entity, specifically because Pope Clement VII had refused to grant the king an annulment from his wife of 24 years, Catherine of Aragon. Out of Catherine's six pregnancies, five resulted in the children being stillborn, and the sole surviving child, Mary (later Queen Mary I), was not a male heir as Henry would have preferred. He would go on to have six different wives, and each marriage ended in either an annulment or death. Henry went to great lengths to avoid having to secure a legal divorce since it was believed that he would not be permitted to remarry if one of his unsuccessful marriages had ended this way.

After the death of Edward's father, King George V, he ascended to the throne during a time of great upheaval. World War I had only concluded less than two decades prior, and World War II was on the horizon. While there was some hesitance toward Edward's reign due to a concern for his fascist sympathies, particularly his tacit support for Adolph Hitler and the Nazi Party in Germany, much more controversy stemmed from his relationship with Wallis. At the time he was crowned king, she was still married to her second husband, shipping magnate Ernest Aldrich Simpson. The fact that Edward watched the celebrations of the official proclamation that he was now king from the window of St James's Palace with her by his side made many members of his family, the government, the public, and the press very uncomfortable. They would tolerate him taking her as a mistress who was kept behind closed doors, but parading her around in front of the world was considered highly inappropriate.

During the succession crisis that followed, Edward was essentially presented with three options: drop Wallis and marry someone deemed acceptable to be the wife of the King of Great Britain, marry against their wishes and cause the entire government to resign and trigger a political quagmire, or abdicate the throne. He offered a counter-proposal that he be permitted to remain king and marry Wallis but deny her the title of Queen Consort. He automatically removes it. When the government turned this down, he surprised many by choosing to abdicate.

While George VI, his younger brother who succeeded him, invested Edward with the royal title of Duke of Windsor, this was not necessarily done with kindness. By granting his brother the title of a royal duke, the new king ensured Edward could not run for election in the House of Commons, and being a royal prevented him from giving political speeches in the House of Lords, effectively removing him from any influence over the law and policy-making. Wallis was not granted the right to style herself as "Royal Highness," as would normally be the case with the spouse of a royal duke. At the very least, she was allowed to be called the Duchess of Windsor, but the bad blood and hurt feelings over the resolution of the abdication crisis caused interpersonal problems between the couple and the rest of the Royal Family for years to come.

The Church of England and the British public's condemnation of divorce when it came to royals reared its ugly head again during the dissolution of Charles and Diana's marriage. Rumors had swirled for years about various affairs carried out by both parties, but it was considered unthinkable for the pair to obtain a legal divorce rather than simply carry on with other lovers in private while maintaining a happy, united front for their subjects. As Charles was first in line to inherit the throne whenever his mother, Queen Elizabeth II, passed away, the idea that he would be crowned following a divorce was unacceptable. However, tensions within the marriage became so untenable that Charles and Diana saw no other avenue besides divorce.

Prince Harry

Harry had a front seat to the nasty smear campaign conducted by those in the media more sympathetic to the Royal Family than Diana throughout the duration of his parents' divorce proceedings. He was also keenly aware of the struggles that Wallis experienced as both an "outsider" marrying into the family and an American actress looked down upon by the general public. In a recent documentary about his and Meghan's decision to step back from their royal duties, he explained, "The pain and suffering of women marrying into this institution, this feeding frenzy. I was terrified. I didn't want history to repeat itself. No one knows the full truth. We know the full truth."

The truth is that Meghan embodied the exact type of person that the British media likes to criticize and demonize: a strong, independent woman who married into the Royal Family as an outsider and refused to step in line with the rest, as is expected. Like Wallis, she is a divorced actress from America and a commoner with no familial ties to the gentry or nobility, and like Diana, she is passionate about her charity work and championing good causes, refusing to remain silent just because something is considered controversial. She doesn't view becoming the wife of a prince as the "happily ever after" to a fairytale life—but in addition to finding love, it was an opportunity to use the high-profile and public visibility to shine a light on issues too often ignored by celebrities and politicians, such as mental health awareness.

Due to this, she was being treated just as poorly as both Diana and Wallis, and Harry had no desire to force his wife to suffer in silence when he had the power to do something about it. Everything he experienced throughout his life had shown him what happens to those who rock the boat and are left on their own to be thrown to the sharks. Wallis Simpson had her reputation ruined over it, and Harry's mother died because of it. He would not let his own wife meet the same fate, so he made the difficult decision to step away from his position within the Royal Family. People who can't reconcile the idea that someone would willingly give up the wealth and prestige that comes with being the son of the King of Great Britain decided that the only reason it happened was that he had his wife whispering poisoned words in his ear.

Instead, they should take a look at the lessons he learned merely by living his life and witnessing the horrific treatment of the women he cares about most. It was a self-fulfilling prophecy on the media and public's end—they were overly critical of every move made by Meghan, and when Harry took steps to protect her, they criticized this decision. This mess could have been avoided if people had taken to heart the tragedy that claimed Diana's life. But rolling around in the mud and slinging it at outsiders within the Royal Family is too tempting to ignore; the constant stream of rumor-mongering and gossip columns have become a cottage industry in itself. Wherever there is money to be made, those willing to exploit the situation for financial gain, regardless of who is harmed in the process, will never stop.

CHAPTER 1

The Early Years

The story of Prince Harry really begins at the inception of the relationship between his parents: Charles, Prince of Wales (later King Charles II) and Lady Diana Spencer, Princess of Wales. The pair first met in 1977, when Diana was 16 years old. At the time, Charles was dating her older sister, Sarah Spencer, although this relationship did not last very long. For much of his bachelorhood, Charles was constantly seen with different women, earning himself something of a reputation as a ladies' man. His granduncle, Lord Louis Francis Albert Victor Nicholas Mountbatten, 1st Earl Mountbatten of Burma, even advised him, "In a case like yours, the man should sow his wild oats and have as many affairs as he can before settling down, but for a wife, he should choose a suitable, attractive and sweet-charactered girl before she has met anyone else, she might fall for...it is disturbing for women to have experienced if they have to remain on a pedestal after marriage."

During this period, Charles' most serious girlfriend was Camilla Rosemary Shand (later Camilla Parker Bowles). Their relationship began when Camilla's boyfriend and future husband, Andrew Parker Bowles, broke up with her in order to pursue Charles' sister, Princess Anne. Charles and Camilla appeared to become quite serious, but the relationship ended when he left England in 1973 to join the British Navy. Camilla and Andrew got back together, eventually getting married in 1973. When Charles returned home, he picked right back up with his bachelor lifestyle, but there was growing pressure from the British Royal Family for him to find a proper wife and settle down.

After the death of Lord Mountbatten, Charles entered a brief period of depression. His granduncle had been a great source of guidance and support, but now that he was gone, the Prince of Wales felt somewhat listless. He started seeing Diana socially, who observed that he had become forlorn and sought to take care of him. This care eventually blossomed into a relationship, and by 1980, she was accompanying him during his visits to Scotland in the summer. However, while there was rampant speculation in the media about the precise nature of their relationship, Charles appeared disinclined for it to progress any further while still continuing to carry on in public with her.

Prince Philip, Charles' father, took notice that the rumors swirling around his son and Diana were beginning to take on a scandalous tone. Fearing the harm this could ultimately do to the young 19-year-old woman's public and social reputation, he sat Charles down and advised the Prince of Wales to make a firm decision on marriage. Philip's point was that the courtship had gone on long enough, and it was no longer appropriate to merely be dating without taking steps toward the altar. If Charles did not want to marry her, it was time to let her go. Instead, Charles interpreted the advice as his father's way of telling him to initiate a marriage to Diana immediately.

Charles proposed in February of 1981, although the couple hid this fact from the press for two and a half weeks. On July 29th, 1981, the 32-year-old Charles married Diana, who was 13 years his junior, at St

Paul's Cathedral in London. By this point, Queen Elizabeth II had been on the throne for 29 years, and the expectation was that he would someday be king and Diana would be his Queen Consort. Unfortunately, the age difference between the pair, which didn't seem to affect their relationship prior to the wedding, slowly began to cause a rift to open up between them. While Charles had spent much of his youth cavorting with numerous women and exploring the world, Diana was only just entering adulthood.

When the magic of becoming a princess and having a fairytale wedding witnessed by 750 million people around the world wore off, the reality of Diana's new life began to settle in. She was effectively trapped in a gilded cage, surrounded by the pomp and opulence afforded to royals, but unable to step foot outside her home without being hounded by the media and the general public. She and her husband were at very different places in their lives when they married, but as the future king's wife, Diana was expected to start having children immediately. One year later, the couple's first son, Prince William, was born, giving the United Kingdom its next heir to the throne.

Following William's birth, troubles between Charles and Diana bubbled to the surface, particularly when it came to the subject of extramarital affairs. Charles had reconnected with Camilla, who was having difficulties in her own marriage. Similarly, as Charles became increasingly emotionally unavailable, Diana sought out comfort in the arms of other men. This caused a great deal of tension between the spouses, although they did their best to shield these problems from the outside world. Putting on a united front and expressing the image of a happy family was paramount to preserving the reputation of the Royal Family, so that was their priority, rather than making any genuine attempts to fix the relationship.

On 15 September 1984, Diana gave birth to her second child, Henry Charles Albert David, known to friends and family as "Harry," while the media and general public typically referred to him as "Prince Harry." At the time of his birth, Harry's father, Charles, was still the Prince of Wales, as his grandmother, Elizabeth II, was in the 32nd year of her long reign as Queen of the United Kingdom and other

Commonwealth Realms. He was delivered in the Lindo Wing of St Mary's Hospital, a National Health Service (NHS) hospital located in the Paddington area of the City of Westminster, a borough of Inner London. The young prince's christening took place on December 21st, 1984, in a ceremony overseen by Robert Runcie, the Archbishop of Canterbury at the time.

As was the usual custom with children of royal birth, Harry was named after previous prestigious members of the ruling class of the United Kingdom: there were eight kings named Henry from 1100-1509 CE; Charles was his father's name; Albert was common to name in the family, including the husband and son of Queen Victoria, and Harry's grandfather (who reigned under the name King George VI); and David, the name of the patron saint of Wales, Saint David, in reference to his mother and father's titles of the Prince and Princess of Wales. Unfortunately, trouble in the marriage between Charles and Diana had been brewing for some time, although throughout Diana's pregnancy with Harry, the couple had managed to somewhat repair the rift, if only temporarily.

The Biography

When Diana discovered that she would have another boy, she tried hiding this fact from her husband. He had been keen to have a girl as their second child, and in an effort to avoid undermining the progress the pair was making in their relationship, she concealed his gender until Charles discovered it for himself following the birth. She'd hoped that once Harry was born and her husband saw him for the first time, Charles would ultimately prove to be delighted at having another son. Instead, almost the opposite occurred. Upon discovering his new child's gender, Charles lamented, "Oh God, it's a boy. And he's even got red hair."

Both of these comments were gutting to Diana. Charles would later attempt to explain away his dismay as a mere joke, but it didn't feel that way to his wife, particularly at the moment. The second part of the comment, referring to Harry's famous status as a "ginger," was also taken by Diana as an insult. Her family had many redheaded members, including former British Prime Minister Winston Churchill. Both Diana and Churchill were descended from Charles Spencer, 3rd Earl Spencer, and Anne Churchill, Charles Spencer's wife. The fact that James Hewitt, a man with whom Diana had engaged in an extramarital affair that ended two years prior to Harry's birth, was also a redhead may have also influenced the way Diana interpreted her husband's words. While it was impossible for Hewitt to have been Harry's biological father, Diana felt that Charles still meant it as a way to needle her about her infidelity.

Despite Charles' insistence to his wife that what he said was a joke, it wasn't the only time he brought up the subject of his preference for the child's gender prior to the birth. On the day of Harry's christening, Charles told Diana's mother, Frances Shand Spencer, "We were so disappointed. We thought it would be a girl." This did not sit well with Frances, who reported the Prince of Wales's words to her daughter, which ignited another fight between the spouses—once more a regular occurrence, as it had been before Diana's pregnancy. Something inside Diana snapped, and she would later state in interviews that this was the moment she realized her marriage was effectively over. However, it would be another 12 years before the couple would officially get a divorce.

The Biography

The implosion of Charles and Diana's relationship meant that Diana poured all of her efforts into her charity work and raising her two boys. William and Harry were her pride and joy, and she was determined to ensure they would have the same e types of experiences as other children, regardless of their status within British society. Diana also wanted to instill in them the attitude and sense of responsibility that she held, preventing them from becoming spoiled or holding themselves above the average British citizen. The importance she placed on civic duty and using one's lofty position to help others is something that would remain with both of her children, even long after she was gone.

When Harry was about 8 months old, he made his first trip abroad, accompanying his parents and older brother during a trip to Italy in their capacity as members of the British Royal Family. They met with Italian President Sandro Pertini during a luncheon he hosted at Quirinale Palace, where Diana delighted the other guests with stories about her newborn son. However, some observers noted the tension between her and Charles, and he offered very little indication that he was equally pleased with the latest extension to the family as his wife. In fact, when actress Monica Vitti made a joke to Charles about how he must have been over the moon to have a second son instead of a daughter, he gave an awkward smile and a nod before walking away in a huff.

As was customary, the Royals traveled with a cadre of bodyguards, assistants, and childcare workers. Despite this, Diana tried to spend as much time with William and Harry as she could, usually during the rare periods when she wasn't expected to attend official functions or perform her duties as the Princess of Wales. Even though Harry was far too young to really understand where he was or what was going on, she brought him to several notable Italian landmarks, regaling both William and the infant with historical tales concerning the sites. It was noted that Harry seemed to take particular delight in Rome's Trevi Fountain, giggling merrily as the water splashed down from the feet of the imposing figure of Oceanus, the ancient Greek Titan of myth.

Harry's education commenced at the Minors Nursery School (formerly Mrs. Mynors Nursery School) in London, which was run by Mrs. Jane Mynors. William had also attended the school, and Mynors was known to have a great deal of affection for the princes. He began attending the school the day after his third birthday and was even photographed by the British media being escorted into the building by Mynors herself. Years later, Mynors recalled him fondly as a bright, funny, and inquisitive child lacking the types of behaviors one might normally associate with a prospective heir to the throne. William had made headlines when he started there, being the first royal prince to go to a private nursery school, and Harry was the second.

Even at such a young age, he endured a phenomenon that would become all too prevalent by the time he was a teenager: being negatively compared to his older brother. Harry was in a peculiar position as the second son of the presumptive heir to the throne. While it was unlikely that he would ever become king, the abdication crisis from the early part of the 20th century was still recent enough to remain in living memory. Should anything happen to Charles, both William and Harry would move up in the line of succession, and if something happened to William before he had any children, Harry would inherit the expectation of becoming king. Due to this, plenty of attention was given to Harry's development, despite the chances that he would ever actually sit on the throne being relatively slim.

The expectations placed upon William and Harry as children may have had an influence on their personalities. William was often said to be a serious, dutiful child, while Harry was more playful and carefree. This resulted in Harry tending to get in trouble more than his elder sibling. These were the types of minor transgressions that just about every child goes through while growing up, but because Harry was a high-ranking member of the Royal Family, the constant spotlight on him caused these incidents to be blown out of proportion by the press. When he got into a brief tussle with another student, the newspapers declared him a "Wild Child." Later, a foolish but harmless prank where he dumped yogurt into a friend's knapsack had the media questioning whether he had undiagnosed psychological issues.

Following two years at the nursery school, Harry joined William at Wetherby School in Notting Hill, London. Diana accompanied the boys on Harry's first day, just as she had done on William's first day in

The Biography

1987. William looked after his younger brother during their time together at the pre-preparatory school, ensuring that Harry always had somebody he trusted nearby in case of any problems. According to palace insiders, this was when the bond between the brothers began to form, as they were sharing a school and old enough to notice how other people treated them a bit differently from everyone else.

During the spring of 1988, an overzealous photographer showed up outside the schoolyard one day and attempted to snap some photos of the princes as they played. This was in violation of the unofficial "social contract" between the Royal Family and the media that stipulated the children would be left alone if they were occasionally brought out for public appearances where they could be photographed. Harry was still too young to understand what was happening, but William recognized that the man taking pictures was both there for the princes specifically and doing something he shouldn't have been doing. William quickly escorted Harry back inside the school while an administrator contacted the authorities to deal with the intrusive photographer.

In 1990, William left Wetherby to attend Ludgrove School, a preparatory boarding school located in Berkshire near Eton College. Harry continued on at Wetherby for two more years and once again joined his older brother at Ludgrove when he turned 8 years old. During the summer breaks, both boys received private tutoring and began to take part in more functions involving the Royal Family. Around this time, Harry was initiated into the tradition of hunting near the grounds of Balmoral Castle, an estate in Aberdeenshire, Scotland, that Queen Elizabeth II used as a summer home. Harry quickly took a liking to the sport of hunting and was gifted the first of many guns to begin what would later become an extensive collection.

In 1991, Harry again went abroad with Charles, Diana, and William, this time to tour Canada. Tellingly, the couple made the decision to attend numerous functions separately, although any news in the press about marital troubles was consistently dismissed by Buckingham Palace insiders. Harry had turned 7 years old shortly before the trip and was a much more visible presence when the family went out in public. While in Toronto, Charles attended an engagement at the Inco nickel mine, while Diana met with patients in the cancer treatment ward at a local medical center. Meanwhile, the two young princes were taken on a secretive outing to the Royal Ontario Museum and the famous CN Tower.

Charles had alluded to his sons' activities during this time, telling a crowd of well-wishers, "They have a chance, I hope, of finding out a great deal more about the parts of Canada that we can't always reach on these occasions." Yet it was Diana who was the driving force behind the children having this opportunity, as she was adamant that they get to do typical "touristy things" while in Canada rather than remain under lock and key at the hotel or making public appearances. Harry was very interested in an exhibit about his grandmother, Elizabeth, that had been added to the museum around the same time he was born. It was one of the first occasions where he saw her presented as almost a figure of worship by the common folk rather than as just another member of the family.

During Harry's time at Ludgrove, especially after William had departed for Eton, much more media attention was focused on the rapidly deteriorating marriage of Charles and Diana. While there had been problems right from the start, the last decade of their relationship was fraught with cheating, emotional manipulation, and explosive fights. Diana's public focus remained on advancing her causes, while privately, she engaged in an affair with a man named John Gilbey. Their relationship was made public in 1992 by The Sun, a tabloid newspaper that dubbed the scandal "Squidgygate," referring to the pet nicknames of "Squidgy" and "Squidge" used by Gilbey for Diana. The bulk of the surreptitiously recorded phone calls between the pair occurred during the late 1980s.

The whole Squidgygate affair began in January of 1990, when a 70-year-old man from Abingdon, England, named Cyril Reenan, accidentally intruded upon a phone conversation taking place between Diana and Gilbey. He would use a homemade non-commercial radio device to eavesdrop on frequencies that carried audio communications and recorded what he found in order to amuse himself and his wife. Despite his claims that he considered erasing the recording or burning the tape, he instead called The Sun and turned it over in exchange for an undisclosed amount of money. Later, Reenan would insist that his first instinct was to bring the tape to Diana and warn her that her conversations could be listened in on, but after deciding he wouldn't get an audience with her, he chose to sell the tape to the tabloid.

In September of 1992, The Sun also obtained a recording made by a 25-year-old woman from Oxfordshire, England, named Jane Norgrove. She claimed to have taped the very same phone conversation as Reenan on New Year's Eve of 1989. According to her, the tabloid offered to buy the tape after she contacted them about it, but she refused. Her reasoning for coming forward so long after the story broke was that she wanted to "clear up" confusion over the matter due to the allegation that the scandal was concocted by palace insiders to smear Diana's name. Most surveillance experts opined that two different sources located over 100 miles apart just happening to record the exact same conversation at the exact same time purely by chance was highly unlikely. While Norgrove has publicly maintained that she was not part of a campaign to harm Diana's reputation, her claims and their timing are incredibly suspect.

Squidgygate became a black mark on the reputation of the Royal Family, airing out their dirty laundry in a very public forum. People were divided in their reactions to the news—some derided Diana as an immoral opportunist, merely using her royal husband for status while sleeping around with common folk, while others viewed her as a victim of societal pressures, trapped in a loveless marriage with a much older man who used her as an incubator for the future heir to the throne. The security of communications going in and out of Buckingham Palace was brought to the forefront of the public consciousness. While in this case, the only thing recorded was a private conversation between Diana and her lover, the ease with which Reenan and Norgrove were able to listen in carried with it the implication that spies or foreign intelligence agents might be capable of intercepting government secrets. Beefing up security was on the docket of Parliament's assembly in the immediate aftermath of the scandal.

Around the same time in 1992, Charles and Camilla became embroiled in their own phone call scandal, dubbed "Camillagate" or "Tampongate." The latter, less discreet name came from a point during the call when Charles jokingly suggested the pair might have an easier time cavorting with one another if he was a part of her wardrobe. The conversation began with some suggestive language, including Camilla, noting that Charles was "awfully good at feeling [his] way along."

Charles responded by stating, "Oh, stop! I want to feel my way along you, all over you, and up and down and in and out. Particularly in and out."

"Oh, that's just what I need at the moment..." Camilla said.

"I'll just live inside your trousers or something. It would be much easier," he told his mistress.

She replied by asking, "What are you going to turn into, a pair of knickers?" The two shared a laugh, and she continued, "Oh, you're going to come back as a pair of knickers!"

At this point, Charles answered by saying, "Or, God forbid, a Tampax! Just my luck!"

"You are a complete idiot!" Camilla asserted but then relented, "Oh, what a wonderful idea."

"My luck to be chucked down a lavatory and go on and on forever swirling round on the top, never going down," lamented the Prince of Wales. Camilla ended this part of the conversation by suggesting Charles could return as a "box of Tampax."

Following the two scandals involving Charles and Diana, then-Prime Minister John Major conducted a governmental investigation into the matter and cleared both MI5 and MI6 of any participation in recording the conversations or leaking the tapes to the public. However, Elizabeth found the entire situation so unsettling that she asked MI5 to investigate what really happened. In 2002, Inspector Ken Wharfe, who had once served as Diana's Personal Protection Officer, claimed that as a result of the investigation, MI5 discovered who was actually behind the leaks, and the Royal Family was satisfied that the matter was concluded. While he could not publicly identify the culprits for legal reasons, he did state that it did "lend credence to the Princess' belief, so often dismissed by her detractors, that the Establishment was out to destroy her."

Throughout these scandals, 8-year-old Harry was forced to watch the media eviscerate his parents, exposing their secrets and criticizing their choices. In addition to the stories in the press, Charles and Diana's marriage hurtled toward an inevitable dissolution, even though the very idea of divorce was anathema to the values of the Royal Family. The queen and her husband attempted to intercede on numerous occasions, advising the couple to settle their differences and reconcile for the good of the "Institution," as the entire apparatus of the Royal Family and their many employees were known. They continued to make appearances together, but it became apparent that the many individual functions they went to solo were occurring more frequently.

After Harry completed his education at Ludgrove School, he sat for the entrance exams to attend Eton College and passed, allowing him to follow in William's footsteps once more. Charles and Diana had broken with royal tradition when they decided to send William to Eton instead of Gordonstoun School in Moray, Scotland. However, Diana's father, Edward John Spencer, 8th Earl Spencer (usually styled John Spencer, Viscount Althorp), and brother, Charles Spencer, had both gone to Eton. When it came time to decide where Harry should attend, the Royal Family had him join William. From the ages of 13 to 18, the princes received a comprehensive secondary education that included many extracurricular activities. During their time at Eton, the boys were faced with two major upheavals in their lives in less than two years: the divorce of their parents and the shocking death of their mother.

CHAPTER 2

The Divorce and Death of Princess Diana

It was a typical frosty day on the cusp of winter when Princess Diana gave an interview that would throw the entire Institution of the British Royal Family into turmoil. Host Martin Bashir conducted the interview for his current affairs documentary television program, Panorama. The episode was broadcast on November 20th, 1995, and Diana spoke very frankly about her relationship with Charles and his suitability to become king someday. This interview included coverage of the couple's extramarital affairs. When discussing Camilla, the Princess of Wales noted, "Well, there were three of us in this marriage, so it was a bit crowded."

After the Panorama episode aired, news stories and palace gossip exploded in the press, with people expressing both sympathy and outrage over the infamous interview. Diana was very candid in her admissions concerning the state of her mental health, which was a topic considered extremely taboo at the time. She confirmed some of the rumors that had been swirling around about her, including the fact that she'd been suffering from severe depression, bulimia, and incidents of self-harm, particularly on her arms and legs. Journalists began accusing her of having borderline personality disorder (BPD), but she was never actually diagnosed with it.

Nearly 25 years later, the BBC confessed that Bashir had duped Diana and her brother into giving the revealing interview by forging bank statements to convince them that he'd been in contact with people close to her who were threatening to leak her private struggles. He positioned himself and the interview as being the best way for Diana to get out ahead of the leak and tell her story in her own words. The unethical actions of the "pop journalist" set into motion a series of events that would bring the unsteady foundations of Charles and Diana's marriage crumbling to the ground. However, as this information didn't come to light until 2020, Bashir was able to continue with his despicable brand of journalism until he was forced to resign in 2021.

On December 20th, 1995, it was announced that Elizabeth had sent both Charles and Diana an official letter telling them to get a divorce. The troubles in their marriage, and the public scrutiny it brought to the Royal Family, had become untenable, so the only reasonable solution was for them to go their separate ways. The couple entered negotiations over the legal aspects of the divorce throughout the summer of 1996, and it was finally granted to them on August 28th. As part of the agreement, Diana received a lump-sum payment of £17 million ($26.52 million in 1996), or £30.42 million ($37.3 million) when adjusted for inflation in 2022. She also received a yearly payment of £400,000 ($624,000) or £715,784 ($877,709) in 2022.

In order to help preserve the integrity of the Royal Family, both Charles and Diana were required to sign confidentiality agreements that barred them from speaking about their marriage or divorce in public. The Queen issued a new letters patent that outlined the general rules for handling titles after the divorce of a future monarch. Diana was no longer allowed to be addressed as "Her Royal Highness" but "Diana, Princess of Wales" instead. Because she was the mother of a potential future king, she remained a part of the Royal Family and kept her precedence within it from her time as Charles' wife. Although Diana was saddened to lose her title, William promised that he would return it to her once he took the throne.

As expected, the media hounded Charles and Diana's sons during this controversial period. They were old enough to understand what their parent's divorce meant but still too young to deal with the complicated issues that were being presented in the press. After the fervor over the divorce began to die down, William and Harry were able to return to some sense of normalcy, focusing on their studies and just being regular teenagers. When they weren't at school, they split their time between both parents, who technically shared custody of the children. However, from a strictly legal standpoint, Charles and Diana may not have actually had full custody of the princes.

King George I passed a law in 1717 known as the "Grand Opinion for the Prerogative Concerning the

Royal Family," which was confirmed by ten judges and upheld in a 1772 ruling. It stated that the monarch had the final say in the way that their grandchildren were raised, even if their parents were still alive. This was due to a lifetime of disagreements and bad feelings between George I and his son, so the king wanted to ensure he could secure the future heir to the throne and prevent him from being influenced by George II. While this law has not been exercised in many generations, it remains enshrined in the British legal system. Before any of the children or grandchildren in line for the throne wish to get married, they must first get permission from the reigning monarch. Fortunately, Elizabeth allowed Charles and Diana to continue raising their sons however they saw fit.

Following the chaos in the media during the divorce, things settled down for William and Harry. Much like the unofficial agreement between the Royal Family and the press from when the princes were children, it was settled that the boys would be free to enjoy their time at Eton without interference so long as updates and photo-ops were provided at regular intervals. John Wakeman, the head of the Press Complaints

Commission at the time William began attending Eton, released a statement saying, "Prince William is not an Institution; nor a soap star; nor a football hero. He is a boy: in the next few years, perhaps the most important and sometimes painful part of his life, he will grow up and become a man." Harry was granted the same leeway, known colloquially as the "pressure cooker agreement," when he started classes in 1998.

Free from the constraints of a loveless marriage, both Charles and Diana could now pursue relationships with people they were far more compatible with. Camilla had divorced her husband Andrew in 1995, which meant that there were no more barriers between her and Charles having a proper relationship. He had always considered her the true love of his life, and it wasn't long before they were seen together during public outings. After his experiences with Diana, he took a firmer stance with the rest of the Royal Family when it came to Camilla. There was no room for anyone else in his life. As he told friends and family members, his relationship with her was "non-negotiable." Charles was determined to make things work between them, regardless of how anyone else felt about the future king being with a divorced woman.

While the media had long been critical of Diana, they weren't much kinder to Charles or Camilla. Opinions about where to lay blame for the breakdown of Charles and Diana's marriage began to shift, and since the truth was that Charles had been cheating on his wife as far back as 1986—only two years after Harry was born—much of the responsibility for what happened was placed on Camilla. She was caught in the crosshairs of public disdain, garnering heaps of negative attention from the press. It got so bad that Charles had to hire a public relations expert to help rehabilitate their image and increase their public profile.

Interest in Diana's private affairs became far more rabid after she left Charles. After all, it was highly likely that her son would someday wear the crown, so whoever she chose to share her life with could have an effect on the Royal Family. Starting in 1996, she met a highly respected heart and lung surgeon named Hasnat Ahmad Khan after being invited to a social function by politician and former cricketer Imran Ahmed Khan Niazi, a relative of Hasnat. During their courtship, Diana often lied to the press about the true nature of their relationship, as Hasnat was an intensely private person who did not wish to have his name and face plastered all over the British media. The longer it went on, the harder it became to keep the truth a secret, which began to strain the couple.

After two years, things came to a head, and Diana and Hasnat's relationship ended. Those close to the pair still disagree on exactly whose decision it was to call it quits. Some of Diana's friends recall that Hasnat broke things off with her, and she was quite distraught over the dissolution of their relationship. However, Hasnat himself would later state that it was Diana's decision. This was in part due to the intrusion of the media, which had caused problems between the two, as well as pressure from Diana's mother, who was allegedly against Diana dating a Muslim. Whether this was true or not, Diana and her mother were estranged for the rest of her life.

While their parents attempted to build new lives for themselves following the divorce, William and Harry were often asked to comment on the latest rumors concerning who Charles and Diana were dating. The official position of the palace communications officials was not to comment on any salacious gossip in the press, and the princes were instructed to do the same. However, their constant badgering caused a visible strain on the boys, who often reacted with disdainful expressions as they tried to push past the barrage of photographers and paparazzi. There was also a significant interest in the princes' dating lives, especially William's, as he neared the age of majority. Whenever he was spotted with a female companion, questions were raised about them being friends or something more.

Unfortunately, William and Harry suffered one of the most tragic events anyone could ever experience when Diana was killed on August 31st, 1997. The death of their beloved mother tore the prince's world apart. It was especially hard on Harry, who absolutely adored his mother and was very much like her in temperament. However, he was not permitted to show his devastation in public, as such displays of raw emotion were looked down upon as being beneath his station. This created a dissonant image, as he and William greeted photographers and mourners during their mother's funeral with the same smiles plastered on their faces that they wore during all their public appearances.

The tragedy of Diana's death was only augmented by the circumstances surrounding it. She had gone to Paris to spend time with her current romantic companion, Dodi Fayed. Dodi was a film producer and the son of Egyptian billionaire Mohamed Al Fayed. The pair were passengers in a car speeding through the city streets in an attempt to outrun a gaggle of paparazzi chasing them. When their vehicle reached the Pont de l'Alma Tunnel, Henri Paul, their driver, lost control of the car and smashed into the side of the tunnel at high speed. Diana, Dodi, and Henri were killed upon impact. Another passenger, Trevor Rees-Jones, managed to survive the accident but suffered a serious head injury. Mohamed had hired Rees-Jones to serve as a bodyguard for his son, as he had feared the increased negative attention that Dodi's relationship with Diana had brought.

Losing Diana at the all-too-young age of 36 caused a major shift in the way the media depicted her. There was a worldwide outpouring of grief and support for the late Princess of Wales. Mourners came from far and wide to share the pain of her death with the

The Biography

Royal Family, which included mountains of flowers and other tokens of affection being left at a memorial for Diana. Famed musician Elton John released an updated version of his song "Candle in the Wind," originally written as a tribute to the late actress Marilyn Monroe. This new version was dedicated to Diana and helped the nation to express their sadness at losing such a bright flame of tireless activism.

Much of Diana's time after her marriage to Charles was spent promoting causes she felt strongly about and advocating for those who didn't have a way for their voices to be heard. She championed those affected by the AIDS crisis, which had gained a significant amount of attention in the late 1980s and early 1990s. A visit to the London Middlesex Hospital's HIV/AIDS unit in 1987, where she was photographed shaking hands with a man afflicted with AIDS, made an enormous impact on the way the general public perceived the disease. During that time, there was a lot of misinformation or misunderstanding about the ways HIV and AIDS were transmitted—with many people treating anyone who had it as pariahs, refusing to even go near them. The fact that such a revered public figure showed no hesitation in having physical contact with an AIDS patient helped to begin the long process of destigmatizing the disease, showing that there was no reason not to treat these patients like normal people.

Another cause close to Diana's heart was the removal of dangerous debris left over from warfare, especially landmines. She was a patron of the charity known as HALO Trust and made numerous trips to locations like Angola and Bosnia and Herzegovina. While touring the Huambo province in Angola in January of 1997, she donned a flak jacket and protective gear, then made a televised walk across a precarious minefield to help raise global awareness about the problem. Around 7,000-13,000 landmine-based casualties were reported each year throughout the 1990s and 2000s, and Diana's historic walk brought a great deal of attention to the matter. She was commended for risking her life on behalf of the victims, and her actions were a major factor in the signing of the Ottawa Treaty in 1997, where 164 nations agreed to ban the use of anti-personnel landmines.

Regardless of one's feelings about Diana's personal life, it is undeniable that she was an incredible force for good in this world. Her activism positively impacted millions of people around the world, but it also made an indelible mark on her children's lives. As they got older, both William and Harry did their best to carry on their mother's legacy, establishing charities and taking up causes to help those in need. However, William's responsibilities as an heir to the throne meant that he did not have as much free time to dedicate to his activism as Harry could. Harry really dove headfirst into taking up the torch Diana left behind. But this didn't happen overnight—it would take years before he was finally in a place in his life where he had gained the maturity to follow in his mother's footsteps. Until then, he was just trying to find his place in the world and mourn the passing of the wonderful woman who had given birth to him.

After it was discovered that the paparazzi had played a significant role in Diana's death, an international dialogue began concerning the unpleasant reality that now surrounded celebrities and politicians, but especially the members of the Royal Family. Every single day of their lives, the royals would take one step out their front door and immediately be bombarded by a herd of amoral "journalists" and "photographers." These people went to any length to get a candid picture or shred of information about the Royal Family. This included hiding out near locations where the royals expected to have privacy and digging through their garbage for scraps of evidence that could be spun to fit whatever narrative their tabloid was peddling.

The most tragic aspect of Diana's death was how it was completely avoidable. The media and the public felt entitled to pry into every nook and cranny of the Royal Family's lives, and the appetite for rumors and gossip fueled an entire industry of invading the royals' privacy. This sense of entitlement only got worse as it became easier to take pictures, transmit them to a news outlet, and print, broadcast, or post their outlandish speculations for public consumption. So long as the people ate it up, the media continued to provide them with the shameless rumor-mongering that titillated the masses.

The relationship between the media and the Royal Family was significantly strained in the aftermath of Diana's death. For a brief period, the spotlight was shining on the cretins who sought to exploit the Royal Family for financial gain. Some news outlets paid tens or hundreds of thousands of pounds for pictures or rumors concerning people like Diana, Charles, William, and Harry. The boys had to return to school to continue their education, but it was a difficult time for both of them. Losing their mother at such a young age profoundly affected the rest of their lives, and even today, it isn't difficult to see parts of her emerge from them.

By the summer of 2003, Harry had completed the standard secondary education at Eton and finished two Advanced Level (A-Level) courses. While at school, he participated in several different sports, being described as a "top-tier athlete." His primary sports were rugby and polo, which both had strong traditions in Great Britain that dated back centuries. Harry was a fairly large young man, towering over many other students at 6'1" and about 160 pounds (185.42 cm and 73 kg). Besides playing sports, he also kept in shape by using the school's workout facilities and cut an impressive figure on the pitch. Now at the age of 19, the media hounded Harry, declaring him one of the most eligible bachelors in the world.

However, he was still considered second to William, who maintained a higher position within the public's imagination.

William first met his future wife, Catherine Elizabeth "Kate" Middleton, in 2001 while the pair were studying together at the University of St Andrews. By the time Harry finished at Eton, William and Kate were living together at Balgove House, an estate just off campus, with two other roommates. The British media covered their relationship in the same way his mother had been when she was dating Charles. Although they broke up briefly, they were back together and going strong by the time they graduated. Gossip and speculation started to build around their relationship, with many asking whether Kate might become the Queen of Great Britain someday.

Meanwhile, Harry was living his life in a manner, not unlike his father. He was a consummate bachelor, and there were constant stories linking him to many women. As the media's intrusion upon his private affairs ramped back up, Harry took a more combative approach to the paparazzi. In his mind, they had essentially murdered his mother, and he didn't hide the way that he felt about them. In October of 2004, he got into an altercation with a photographer after leaving a nightclub in London's West End. The crowd of photographers swarmed him as soon as he exited the club, snapping pictures of the young man as quickly as they could manage. One shoved his camera right in Harry's face, and he lashed out, connecting with the paparazzo's face, leaving him with a cut lip.

As expected, the media leaped on the story, depicting Harry as an out-of-control, spoiled prince. Nobody seemed to want to reflect on the fact that day after day, he was faced with pushy, amoral publicity hounds who haunted his every step. They were like a suffocating shadow that followed him everywhere he went. These were the same people who had chased his mother down just for an opportunity to get a snapshot of Diana with her rumored lover, which they could then turn around and sell for a major windfall. Now, these gremlins were coming after him, and as a 20-year-old man filled with pent-up sadness and rage, it was only a matter of time before he snapped. It was actually a fairly impressive show of restraint on Harry's part that the only injury suffered by the paparazzo was a minor flesh wound.

Working through the pain of losing Diana while having his every action examined under a microscope and picked apart by hordes of strangers didn't help make things easier for Harry. Understandably, he made mistakes and regrettable decisions, just like any other young man navigating the treacherous seas of the path from childhood to adulthood. He experimented with recreational drugs—mainly cannabis—and indulged in partying and drinking. While having a rebellious streak in one's youth is a common form of self-expression and a typical experience in the modern world, most people are allowed to make their mistakes, learn from them, and move on. Yet for Harry, every little thing he did was permanently enshrined by the media.

Lacking the guidance of his mother, the young prince had nobody to turn to during this period of his life. He was undoubtedly suffering from mental health issues, particularly anger and depression that stemmed from the loss of Diana. But while Diana herself was incredibly understanding and sympathetic when it came to treating mental health problems, since she had gone through her own ordeals, the rest of the Royal Family held a vastly different view on the matter. At that time in Great Britain, the expectation placed on individuals who came from a higher social class than the average citizen was to maintain a "stiff upper lip." Actually, engaging with these issues and seeking treatment through therapy or other means was out of the question. Harry was told to "act like a proper prince," pushing any intrusive thoughts or feelings deep down inside him and adopting an air of regal stoicism.

Unlike William, there was far more pushback when it came to the media and the general public's relationship with the Royal Family from Harry. Part of the invisible contract between the royals and the people was that the potential heirs to the throne would maintain a respectable image to represent the demeanor of the entire nation. It was embarrassing for them to have a prince who behaved like a normal person instead of reflecting the type of immaculate behavior associated with an elevated social position. Members of the Royal Family were seen as being superior to the common folk, so naturally, there was a significant amount of pressure placed upon them to never slip up, especially in public. No matter how difficult a situation they found themselves in, the royals were not permitted to act like normal people—they needed to be better.

It's easier to understand the conditions in which Harry was growing up now than it was back then. The advent of social media, and the idea that everything you do as a child, teenager, or young adult is documented, shared, and preserved for all time, was not a typical experience for the average person. It was unique to individuals in positions of high visibility, like child actors or the kids of famous celebrities and politicians. Nowadays, anyone can have a picture posted of them during a moment in their life when they made a poor decision, and these images and stories will follow them for the rest of their lives. People's mistakes are etched into a permanent record, and no matter how much they might develop and grow, there will always be evidence that they were mere humans once upon a time.

The Biography

It's a daunting thought for modern youths that a stupid, short-sighted choice made as a teenager or young adult can haunt them as they enter the professional world or attempt to build relationships and families in the future. This was exactly what Harry experienced as he grew up, but there was far less understanding of just how much of a strain this could put on a person. Social media outlets such as Twitter or Facebook allow anyone to say whatever they want about anything they desire, and their words can reach hundreds or thousands, or millions of people across the world. In the mid to late 1990s, though, this experience was limited to individuals like the Royal Family. But while Harry seemed to be getting nothing but negative press coverage, the opposite was true for his brother William.

CHAPTER 3
The Heir and the Spare

The relationship between William and Kate became more serious after the pair had finished their studies at university, while Harry continued to make headlines for the wrong reasons. A minor controversy erupted after Harry was photographed attending a costume party in Wiltshire, England. The party's theme was "Colonial and Natives," and Harry arrived dressed as an officer of the Nazi German Afrika Korps. His costume included an armband emblazoned with a swastika, the infamous symbol of the Nazi Party. This was viewed as incredibly insensitive to the Jewish people, who had suffered greatly under the Nazi Party's genocidal policies, particularly their imprisonment and executions all across Germany, Austria, and Poland in concentration camps during the Holocaust. This caused one media outlet to declare him "Hellraiser Harry."

The Biography

After the controversy, Harry did some introspection over the incident, which included visiting a rabbi and Holocaust survivor in Germany. Their discussion opened his eyes to the reality of what occurred in the 1930s and 1940s to the Jewish people and why it was considered so disrespectful to wear a Nazi uniform, making light of the situation. Harry came out of the controversy with a greater awareness of how his actions could impact others, even when he didn't necessarily mean to cause offense. He realized that as a person in a highly visible position in society, he had a responsibility to consider what message he was sending to the public when he stepped outside of his home.

Although Harry was third in line for the throne, there was the expectation that William's future children would ultimately supersede him in the line of succession. The old concept that monarchs needed to have multiple children so there would be an "heir and a spare" seemed to apply to Harry, who was considered the "spare." He was a backup in case Charles and William were somehow unable or unwilling to take the throne when the time came. However, this left him in something of a limbo state—it wasn't likely that he would ever be king, especially since it looked as though William and Kate's relationship was headed toward marriage, but he also was dissuaded from pursuing any activities that would put his life on a course that took him too far away from the Royal Family.

Around 2003, the media picked up a story involving Harry's romantic life when he began dating Natalie Pinkham, a TV sportscaster who reported on Formula One racing. They first met during the 1999 Rugby World Cup in Wales. Four years after this meeting, the pair became an official couple. She was six years older than him, which caused some consternation, as Harry was still only 19 years old while she was 25 years old. This relationship didn't last very long, fizzling out within a few months. It would be 13 years before they saw one another again, and Natalie happened to be pregnant with her second child at the time.

Later in 2003, Harry began a relationship with a woman named Cassie Summer. She was only a year older than him and had previously dated actor and musician Russell Brand. They met in a bar while both were with friends, and according to Cassie, he was sitting at a private table and gazed at her while she stood at the bar. They made eye contact, and then Harry invited her to join him. This relationship was even briefer than the one with Natalie. Palace sources claim that there was never anything serious between them and that they were just having fun, as people their age often did.

Once Harry had finished his schooling, he decided to take a gap year. He went to Australia, where he worked on a cattle station as a "jackaroo," which allowed him to gain practical experience in how a cattle station is operated. Later that year, he traveled to Lesotho in South Africa to help orphaned children. Diana had also spent time in Lesotho, so Harry followed in his mother's footsteps. While in Lesotho, he met and became close with Prince Seeiso, the younger brother of the country's king, Letsie III. The two bonded over their shared passion for charity work and activism and the fact that they had both lost their mothers. Another aspect that connected them was their position as the younger brothers of a king or future king. They could each relate to the stress and pressure of simultaneously being a royal in line for the throne and a backup who would only become king if tragedy struck their families.

Harry and Seeiso formed a charity called Senteble, dedicated to helping orphaned children in Lesotho. During his stay there, Harry presented himself very modestly, wearing casual clothing and assisting the locals with labor tasks. The people were impressed by his work ethic and humble attitude since he did not give off the air of someone from the highest tier of British society. By the end of his time in Lesotho, Harry had come to be quite fond of the people, and he and Seeiso stated that they viewed each other as brothers. When a reporter asked him if his mother's activism influenced his decision to provide aid to the orphans of Lesotho, he replied that her actions had a huge impact on him, and he was doing his best to honor her memory by undertaking projects he believed she would have done herself.

In 2005, Harry decided he wanted to join the military. His father and grandmother were not thrilled with the idea, but he pushed them to allow him to attend the Royal Military Academy Sandhurst. Many members of the Royal Family had military experience, including Charles, Lord Mountbatten, Charles' beloved late granduncle, and Charles' father and grandfather. Charles had been an aviator in the Royal Navy, and Harry had expressed an interest in learning how to fly, but the major difference between Charles and Harry was that there was no major war occurring when Charles was in the military. The conflicts in Afghanistan and Iraq were in full swing by 2005, which meant that if Harry enlisted, there was a good chance he would end up seeing combat. That was an undesirable situation for a potential heir to the throne as far as the Royal Family was concerned.

In the end, Harry managed to get his way, and after spending a year at the Academy's officer training program as "Officer Cadet Wales," he was commissioned as a cornet (the equivalent of a second lieutenant) in a regiment of the British Army's Household Cavalry known as the Blues and Royals. His unit was scheduled for deployment to Iraq in 2007, but a public debate ensued over whether it was appropriate or safe for the prince to be placed in combat when he was an important component of the Institution. Until William had a child, Harry remained third in line to inherit the throne. Both Elizabeth and Charles were relatively old, so it wouldn't be a surprise if one or both of them died. If that happened, he would move up to first or second in line.

Members of the British government thought it would be better if the Royal Family used their influence to ensure Harry received a posting in a non-combat capacity, keeping him well away from the front lines. In response, Harry issued a statement saying that if he was prevented from being deployed to the front lines like any other soldier, he would leave the army, as he didn't want special treatment and had trained to fight for his country. He had no desire to be sent somewhere safe while the rest of his regiment was put in harm's way. This display of solidarity greatly endeared him to his fellow soldiers and the members of the government who had objected to him being sent to the front lines relented.

William also decided to join the military, and in 2006, he entered the Royal Military Academy Sandhurst, just like his younger brother. He was commissioned as a lieutenant and was called Lieutenant Wales in his capacity as an officer. Following his training at Bovington Camp in Dorset, England, William joined the Blues and Royals, the same regiment as Harry, where he was put in command of an armored reconnaissance unit. Although his younger brother was reluctantly permitted to see active combat, this was out of the question for William. Instead, he trained with the Royal Navy and Royal Air Force to become a helicopter pilot. He earned a commission as a sub-lieutenant in the navy and a flying officer in the air force.

Things seemed to change for Harry when he began dating Chelsy Yvonne Davy, the daughter of a successful businessman from South Africa. They had met 18 months before his 21st birthday, which he revealed to the public during a television interview conducted by Sky News. Besides revealing his girlfriend, he also apologized for the incident with the Nazi uniform. However, he made it clear that he held great contempt for how the media portrayed himself, his family, and Chelsy, saying, "There is truth, and there are lies, and unfortunately, I cannot get the truth across."

Surprisingly, he also complimented Camilla, telling the interviewer that he and William both "loved her to bits." He went on to state, "She has always been very close to William and me. But no, she's not the wicked stepmother...she's a wonderful woman, and she's made my father very, very happy. Everyone's happy. Everyone's fine." Charles and Camilla had gotten married on April 9th of that year. It had been a small, intimate ceremony, as the Royal Family was all too cognizant of how she was perceived by the public and did not wish to make a big deal about the marriage. Harry's acceptance of Camilla went a long way in changing some minds about her, although she was still regularly criticized by the media.

In the spring of 2007, General Sir Richard Dannett, who was the head of the British Army at that time, made a public announcement informing the public that Harry was scheduled to be deployed in the summer to the Maysan Governorate in Iraq, where he would be part of the patrol units. Unfortunately, outside factors conspired to force the prince away from the front lines. When the insurgent forces discovered that Harry was set to join the rest of his regiment in Iraq, they put out a statement claiming they'd placed a huge bounty on Harry's head, and they would do everything possible to kill him. Fearing that his presence would now place his fellow soldiers in more danger than they already were, the decision was made to reassign him to a non-combat role.

Harry was disappointed by this decision, but in light of the threats, they understood and accepted it. He was sent to the Canadian Forces Base Suffield in Alberta, Canada instead, where he was to train alongside both the Canadian Forces and British Army. This training was meant to give him additional skills and preparation for eventual deployment to Afghanistan. A media blackout on information concerning Harry was issued, as it was feared that if the enemy forces learned about the plans for him, they would attempt to assassinate him.

The British Army secretly deployed Harry to Helmand Province in Afghanistan to serve as a Forward Air Controller in late 2007. He took on regular duties as an officer, insisting that he not be treated differently or shown any favoritism by his superiors. His personable demeanor and down-to-earth attitude went a long way in helping him connect with the men in his unit. During their downtime, they would joke around or play soccer, which allowed Harry to show off his athletic abilities. To the other soldiers, he wasn't Prince Harry—just Cornet Harry Wales.

During a routine patrol with his squad and members of the Brigade of Gurkha, which consisted of Nepalese Gurkha troops, they were ambushed by Taliban insurgents. The group was forced to fend off the attack, and Harry manned one of the machine guns during the battle. The British and Gurkha soldiers managed to successfully repel the insurgents, and Harry was praised for his conduct during the fight. He continued to serve in hostile areas around the province, sharing the risks to his life alongside the rest of his regiment.

While most of the press abided by the blackout, the Australian publication New Idea and the German newspaper *Bild* both had articles revealing the prince's whereabouts. As soon as it became public, the army pulled Harry out of Afghanistan, much to his chagrin. Upon returning to the United Kingdom, he was stationed at the Combermere Barracks, a military installation close to Windsor Castle. He was presented with an Operational Service Medal for Afghanistan in a ceremony led by his aunt, Princess Anne. Chelsy was by his side during the ceremony, ecstatic to have Harry back home. In April of 2008, after having two years of experience as a cornet, he received a promotion to lieutenant.

By serving in Afghanistan, the prince became the first member of the Royal Family since his uncle, Prince Andrew, to see active combat. Andrew had flown helicopters for the Royal Navy and participated in the Falklands War in 1982. This influenced Harry to train as a helicopter pilot, just as his brother and father did. Both princes attended the Defence Helicopter Flying School at the Royal Air Force Shawbury. He had a natural talent as a pilot, a fact that he later ascribed to his penchant for playing video games on the PlayStation and Xbox consoles, which had controllers not too different from a helicopter's weapons systems.

While training to fly, Harry's relationship with Chelsy begins to fall apart. In early 2009, palace officials told the media that the couple had broken up. Later that year, he met Astrid Harbord, a friend of Kate Middleton. Kate introduced Harry to Astrid during a party that she and the brothers attended. Harry was spotted going to clubs with Astrid on a few occasions, but the relationship did not last long. By the summer, they had gone their separate ways. Kate was reportedly a bit miffed at Harry, as he had been the one to end things with Astrid, and she was upset after their breakup.

Around the autumn of 2009, Harry's ex-girlfriend Natalie introduced him to Caroline Flack, a former presenter on the television series *X Factor*. Caroline bestowed the nickname "Jam" upon Harry, explaining that it was a reference to his red hair and the fact that he was very sweet. Things between them were going well at first, but as soon as the media discovered they were dating, the paparazzi came out in droves, hounding the couple everywhere they went. The pressure of constantly being watched by rabid photographers became too much for Caroline. As soon as the story broke that they were together, Caroline felt like she had lost her identity. Caroline was quoted as saying, "Once the story got out, that was it. We had to stop seeing each other. I was no longer Caroline Flack, TV presenter, I was Caroline Flack, Prince Harry's bit of rough."

Despite the distractions in his personal life, Harry completed his training to become a helicopter pilot in 2010. He was presented with a flying brevet by his father, Charles, in a ceremony on May 7th. Around the same time, he was linked to singer/songwriter Mollie King. They attended the Asprey World Class Cup at Surrey's Hurtwood Polo Club together. Unfortunately, Mollie broke the Institution's protocol, speaking freely about the relationship with the press. Anyone who entered a relationship with a member of the Royal Family was expected to simply smile while out in public but never engage with the media. This breach in protocol caused Harry to break up with her, which she bitterly recalled to journalists in 2012.

Following the short-lived relationship with Mollie, Harry was soon spotted with another musician—this time, it was a Norwegian rock star named Camilla Romestrand. According to Romestrand, she spent time with Harry at Clarence House, and he even made her breakfast in bed one morning in an attempt to impress her. In what was quickly becoming a pattern, Harry and Camilla broke things off not long after the relationship began. The media was beginning to comment on Harry's heartbreaker tendencies, comparing him to his father, who was also something of a ladies' man in his youth.

Near the end of 2010, representatives of the Royal Family announced that William and Kate had gotten engaged after he proposed to her while they were in Kenya for some charity work. William aptly gave Kate the same engagement ring that his father had given his mother. They were officially married at Westminster Abbey on 29 April 2011, when the couple became the new Duke and Duchess of Cambridge. Harry served as his brother's best man, while Kate's sister, Pippa Middleton, was her maid of honor. Although there was some mild flirtation between Harry and Pippa, leading to a short-lived spate of speculation that the pair might get together, this ultimately came to nothing.

Pippa experienced what it was like to be at the center of overbearing public scrutiny when a picture was taken from behind of her walking up Abbey's steps as she tended to the train of her sister's dress, setting off a firestorm of attention. Some people became fixated on her rear, which even garnered its own FaceBook page that boasted thousands of members. Others slammed her for supposedly wearing a form-fitting dress to purposely steal attention from her sister. While Pippa took most of these comments in stride, noting that the dress may have been "fitted too well" if there had been any chance of a relationship with Harry prior to the wedding, the uncomfortable amount of focus on her as a tangentially-related member of the Royal Family stomped out any desire to deal with such things permanently.

On April 14th, 2011, a few weeks prior to the wedding, Harry was awarded an Apache Flying Badge. This meant he was certified to pilot the Apache helicopters used by the Royal Navy and Royal Air Force. Two days later, he was promoted to the rank of captain. He was now eligible to take on an active role in the military as a helicopter pilot, but the decision of where to deploy him rested with the senior commanders of the Ministry of Defence. They consulted with Elizabeth, taking her opinion into account when making their final decision. He was sent to California in the United States to receive further gunship training and returned to England for additional instruction in piloting the Apache helicopters after completing that program.

While training back in England, Harry met model and actress Florence Brudenell-Bruce, a woman about a year younger than him who was the daughter of wine merchant Andrew Brudenell-Bruce, 3rd Marquess of

Ailesbury and 9th Earl of Cardigan. Although things went smoothly in the beginning, Florence felt that Harry had a wandering eye. He apparently did not hide his interest in other women, and she believed he was talking to and flirting with people whenever they were apart. Predictably, the relationship didn't last, and Florence would later go on to marry a multimillionaire banker named Henry St George and have a child with him.

Harry completed his additional training with helicopters, and he was deployed back to Afghanistan on September 7th, 2012. He was assigned to Camp Bastion in Helmand Province as part of the 662nd Squadron, 3rd Regiment, Army Air Corps—which contained about 100 soldiers. He had the advantage of already being familiar with the province from his first tour of duty. When his location was again leaked by members of the press, the Taliban reignited their calls for his head. The spokesman for the Taliban, Zabiullah Mujahid, told the media, "We are using all our strength to get rid of him, either by killing or kidnapping. We have informed our commanders in Helmand to do whatever they can to eliminate him." Eleven days later, there was an attack by the Taliban on Camp Bastion that resulted in the death of two US marines. Harry was moved to a secret location immediately after this, and additional security measures were put in place to keep the prince safe.

Despite the risk, Harry continued to fly Apache helicopters in hostile territory. He was faced with Taliban insurgents on numerous occasions and was forced to fire upon them in order to save the lives of both soldiers and innocent civilians caught in the middle of the two forces. He described his experiences in combat situations, asserting that while he and his fellow Apache pilots would use lethal force, when necessary, their presence often served as enough of a deterrent to prevent attacks by the insurgents. His second deployment lasted 20 weeks, double the amount of time as his first tour in Afghanistan. On July 8th, 2013, it was announced that Harry had qualified to become an Apache helicopter commander, gaining another notch in his belt as an accomplished soldier and officer.

William and Kate had their first child together on July 22nd, 2013. Their new son, Prince George, became the third in line to the throne, pushing Harry down to fourth in line. Now that William had a child of his own, it was almost certain that Harry would never become king. However, Harry found this to be liberating, as he was no longer needed as the "spare." He hoped that since the line of succession was more or less secure without him, he would be free to pursue his own destiny independent of his responsibilities to the Royal Family. By this point, he was enthusiastic about his military service and continued to renew his enlistment, turning it into a viable career.

Around the time of his second tour of duty, Harry began dating another actress and model named Cressida Bonas. It was becoming clear that the prince had a type, with the majority of his girlfriend's working in the entertainment industry in some capacity. This relationship was far more serious than the flings he had following his breakup with Chelsy. Harry met Cressida after being introduced to her by his cousins, Princesses Beatrice and Eugenie, the daughters of his uncle, Prince Andrew. As expected, the media picked up on the story, invading Harry's privacy once more. Fortunately, Cressida seemed to deal well enough with the extra attention, which allowed the relationship to continue even after it was found out by the public.

Once Harry's attachment to the Air Army Corps' 3rd Regiment had ended, he returned to England and was stationed at HQ London District in Horse Guards, where he was given a staff officer role. He was placed in a position where he would be responsible for coordinating major projects and commemorative events put on by the army. The most notable of these events was the Invictus Games. This was a sporting competition similar to the Paralympics or Special Olympics, featuring competitors from the military who had been injured during combat. Preparations for the games ramped up in the spring of 2014 when Harry began meeting with potential athletes at Tedworth House in Wilshire, England. There was a huge media push for the Invictus Games, and the prince was interviewed on broadcaster Chris Evans' (not the actor who played Captain America) show for *BBC 2 Radio* about the project. Harry explained that he was essentially coordinating the competition as a full-time job.

The experiences Harry had with fellow soldiers injured in combat while fighting insurgents in

Afghanistan were the impetus for his desire to create the Invictus Games. A later visit to the Warrior Games, a similar competition put on by the Department of Defense for the United States military's wounded soldiers, gave him the confidence that this idea could be equally successful in Great Britain. The Invictus Games were officially announced during a press conference at Potters Field Park in August of 2014, with the games set to take place between September 8th-14th, 2014. In his role as president of the Invictus Games, Harry was present every day, watching the competition from a box seat with other military officials and government figures.

As Harry became more involved in charity work and Cressida put greater focus on her career, it became clear to the couple that they simply wanted different things out of life. They parted on good terms, and in interviews immediately following the end of their relationship, they both complimented one another to the press. The prevailing belief that their split was amicable was challenged several years later, but at the time, it looked as though Harry was just not having the same kind of luck in finding a long-term partner as his brother did. William and Kate had been together for nearly a decade by the time they got married, whereas Harry's longest relationship only lasted about half that length.

After the new year in 2015, Harry took on a larger role in additional charities that support wounded veterans. He began working with the London District's Personnel Recovery Unit, which helped provide injured soldiers with a recovery plan once they were out of immediate care medical facilities. In conjunction with the charity Help for Heroes (H4H), Royal British Legion (RBL), Fisher House Foundation, and the Queen Elizabeth Hospital Birmingham (QEHB), the Battle Back Centre was established for the purpose of assisting those wounded in combat as they returned home and attempted to return to lives as civilians. The Battle Back Centre also helped soldiers suffering from mental health issues, which was something that had been lacking for many years in countries all over the world.

On May 2nd, 2015, Kate gave birth to her and William's second child, a daughter that they named Princess Charlotte. Again, Harry was pushed further down the line of succession, as Charlotte replaced him as fourth in line. This essentially sealed the new line of succession through William, leaving Harry on the outside. While he had no interest in being king, it did leave him somewhat adrift. He was still a member of the Royal Family and the son, brother, and uncle of potential future kings, but he did not possess as high of a position as he once had. With his time in the military soon coming to a close, Harry was going to have to figure out exactly what he wished to do with the rest of his life.

The spring of 2015 saw Harry be seconded to the Australian Defence Force (ADF), taking up residence on bases in Sydney, Darwin, and Perth. He trained with the ADF's 2nd Commando Regiment, taking part in urban operations exercises. Later, he received training with clearance divers from the Royal Australian Navy in counterterrorism techniques and learned how to fly a Black Hawk helicopter. By the summer of that year, he resigned from his short-lived commission and headed back to England, leaving active duty altogether. Upon his retirement from the military, he served two tours of duty in Afghanistan and spent a decade as a member of the armed forces.

Harry's return to England didn't mean he was content to spend his free time relaxing outside of taking up public appearances on behalf of the Royal Family again. In November, he traveled to Lesotho in order to attend the unveiling ceremony of the Mamohato Children's Centre in his role as a founder of Sentebale. While there, he reconnected with Seeiso, whose mother's name was used for the Centre as a way to honor her. After leaving Lesotho, Harry spent time in South Africa, bestowing an insignia from the Order of the Companions of Honour upon Cape Town's archbishop. While there, he also participated in the Sentebale Royal Salute Polo Cup, dusting off his skills from his Eton days. In March 2016, he went to Nepal, where he personally assisted in rebuilding a secondary school that had been destroyed during a recent natural disaster.

Prior to leaving for Africa, Harry was seen in public on several occasions with pop music star Ellie Goulding, who had previously sung at both William and Kate's wedding, and the 2014 Invictus Games. They were spotted at a polo match together, but Goulding was cagey when asked about her relationship with the prince, following protocol by refusing to actually give out any information to the press. Although she may have held out hope that they would reconnect when Harry returned from his trip overseas, their busy schedules made it difficult to find time to meet up. The real nail in the coffin of any potential romance between them came in July 2016 when a friend of Harry's arranged for him to meet with a rising television star named Meghan Markle.

CHAPTER 4

Meghan Markle

Rachel Meghan Markle, known professionally as "Meghan Markle," was born on August 4th, 1981, making her a little over three years older than Harry. Her parents, Thomas Markle, Sr., and Doria Ragland were residing together in Los Angeles, California, at the time of her birth. She is mixed race since her father is Caucasian and her mother is African-American. Although Meghan was Doria's first and only child, Thomas had two significantly older children from a previous relationship named Samantha and Thomas, Jr. The apartment where Meghan spent the first few years of her life was modest, and her half-siblings rarely came to visit the family.

Thomas worked as a lighting director and director of photography in Hollywood, with one of his most notable jobs being on the sitcom *Married...with*

Children, as well as the long-running soap opera *General Hospital*, which garnered him an Emmy award. Doria was a flight attendant, so Meghan was often left at home with Thomas while she was away, and the two became very close. Sadly, when Meghan was 2 years old, her parents separated, and Thomas moved out. Two years later, the couple got divorced, and Meghan relocated with her mother to a carriage apartment on the outskirts of LA.

Even from an early age, Meghan proved that she had strong convictions. At 11 years old, she wrote a letter to Procter & Gamble concerning a recent commercial they'd put out for their Ivory Soap brand. The commercial had a voiceover component that specified their product was a lifesaver for women, implying that only women washed dishes. After several classmates who had viewed the commercial made disparaging comments to Meghan about how a woman's place was in the kitchen, she contacted the company and explained her position, requesting that they change it. To her surprise, she later watched the commercial, only to find that during the voiceover, the line about women had been replaced with a gender-neutral term.

The Biography

For grades 6-12, Meghan attended the all-girls Catholic school Immaculate Heart High School and Middle School in Los Angeles. However, she was raised Protestant, which is a branch of Western Christianity that evolved from the Protestant Reformation in the 16th century, much like Anglicanism in England. While at Immaculate Heart, Meghan participated in many musicals and plays put on by the student body, proving to have a knack for acting. Her interest in film, television, and stage productions was cultivated by her father, who she often visited on the sets where he was working, getting a chance to see how things were done behind the scenes. She even got a small background role in two episodes of *Married...with Children* in 1995. Thomas occasionally helped out with the school productions, lending his expertise in lighting.

In addition to her extracurricular activities, Meghan spent her free time performing volunteer work. She worked at a soup kitchen in the economically poor section of downtown LA known as "Skid Row" and helped out at the local church to distribute food and clothing to those in need. During high school, she got a job at a frozen yogurt shop, waited tables at a restaurant, and served as a reliable babysitter for parents in the area. She was an incredibly bright and diligent student, consistently receiving high marks in her classes, and was accepted into Northwestern University (NU), located in Evanston, Illinois.

Meghan enrolled at NU for the fall semester in 1999, entering their School of Communication, and soon rushed to the sorority Kappa Gamma. Along with her sorority sisters, she volunteered at the charity known as the Glass Slipper Project, which provided dresses, shoes, and other outfit accessories for proms to underprivileged students throughout the state. During her junior year at NU, Meghan won a prestigious internship with the American embassy in Buenos Aires, Argentina, which allowed her to get some practical experience in politics. She also joined the university's study abroad program in Madrid, Spain, for a semester.

In the spring of 2003, Meghan graduated from NU with a double major in theater and international studies, earning her bachelor's degree in both specializations. Although she had considered a career in politics, her passion for acting led her to pursue a career in the entertainment industry instead. She returned to LA, where she started going to open call auditions. During this period, she often found herself being turned down for roles due to her ethnicity, as she was deemed "too white" for African-American characters and "too black" for Caucasian ones. To support herself as she continued to audition, she worked as a freelance calligrapher and taught a class in bookbinding.

In 2002, Meghan booked her first real acting job when she was cast as a nurse named Jill in the soap opera *General Hospital*. While her father had been the lighting director on the same program from 1979 to 1996, he only worked on 72 of the 1,405 episodes produced during that time span, so his connection to the show didn't help her land the role. She continued to book guest spots on different shows, including *Century City, The War at Home, and CSI: NY*. In 2006, she was hired as a model who held "Case #24" in 34 episodes of the game show *Deal or No Deal*. The program was extremely successful, raising her visibility in the entertainment industry.

While getting regular work on a variety of television shows, Meghan was constantly meeting new people involved in the productions. In 2004, she began dating a producer named Trevor Engelson, and they got married on August 16th, 2011, in Ocho Rios, Jamaica. Their marriage didn't last long, and they separated after 18 months. In February 2014, they were granted a no-fault divorce, where the reason for the end of the relationship was given as irreconcilable differences. Engelson later became involved with Bethany Frankel, star of the reality TV series *The Real Housewives of New York City*, but their romance fizzled out, and they only remained connected through a business relationship. He went on to marry a dietitian named Tracey Kurland, an heiress to her father's multi-million dollar fortune, and the couple had two children together.

After her divorce, Meghan had another spate of guest roles and joined the USA Network's original series *Suits*, where she played Rachel Zane, one of the main characters. She remained with the show from 2011 to 2018, performing in the first seven of its nine seasons. During her tenure in the program, she met a celebrity chef and restaurateur named Cory Vitiello. He was based in Ontario, Canada, and Suits filmed most of their program in Toronto, Ontario. The couple moved in together, but they ended their two-year relationship in May 2016.

As her career took off, Meghan sought to use her increasing fame to bring causes close to her heart to the forefront, and she delved deeper into politics. In 2014, she joined the organization One Young World, which promoted young leaders and gave them a platform on the global stage. She participated in the United Nations Women's Conference in 2015, delivering a popular and well-regarded speech to the assembled crowd of thousands. Later, she campaigned on behalf of Democratic candidate Hilary Clinton during the 2016 election season, although Clinton's bid for the Presidency of the United States was unsuccessful, losing to Republican candidate Donald J. Trump.

Early in 2016, Meghan was named as a global ambassador for a Christian relief organization known as World Vision Canada. She went with them to Rwanda, participating in the Clean Water Campaign, which focused on building wells from which clean water could be drawn, allowing the locals a better source of dependable drinking water with greater accessibility than the natural water sources that required much more time to reach. Soon after, she traveled to India and spoke about women's rights, and worked alongside the UN Entity for Gender Equality and the Empowerment of Women. She also penned an article for TIME Magazine on the topic of menstrual health and the stigma surrounding it. By this point in time, she was a very vocal feminist and stayed incredibly busy with her advocacy efforts.

Barely two months after breaking things off with Vitiello, Meghan Markle sauntered off the set of the Suits and into Harry's life. During the summer break in production, she decided to travel to Europe with friends. Late one night, Harry was scrolling through the social media platform Instagram, browsing pictures posted by a friend. In one photo, he noticed another woman posing with his friend and was struck by her beauty. He messaged the friend to ask about the identity of the woman in the picture, and the friend contacted Meghan, alerting her about the interest of her friend "Haz," as she called Harry. Meghan responded positively to the idea of being set up with Harry, so the two coordinated with each other and set a time to have a blind date.

The Biography

Meghan arrived at the restaurant in London where the pair were supposed to meet, but Harry was running late. He'd gotten stuck in traffic and was frantically trying to reach the restaurant, worried that Meghan would think he stood her up. Although he messaged her that he was stuck in traffic, her initial response was one of consternation. It looked to her like Harry was just a typical spoiled rich kid who had no respect for other people's time, showing up late to engagements and expecting everyone else to wait around for him. However, when he finally arrived, he was so flustered and apologetic that Meghan forgave him, and they proceeded with their date.

The two connected almost immediately, finding that they shared quite a few interests. They both had a passion for volunteering and charity work, and it appeared that many of their personal values were closely aligned. Despite how well the date went, Meghan was somewhat reserved in her enthusiasm for Harry. After all, he had an extensive history of dating actresses, but their relationships never lasted very long. She feared that she would become just another ex-girlfriend and was not looking for a fling—especially not one with a prince. Fortunately, their second date went extremely well, and Meghan's concerns were put to rest.

Following their second date, Meghan continued on with her vacation, but she and Harry kept in constant contact with each other. He was scheduled to go to Botswana, Africa, to help with the charity Elephants Without Borders, a conservation group that focused on endangered African elephants. He decided to invite Meghan to join him on the trip but made it clear that this wasn't a vacation. They would be sleeping in a tent and have limited access to the comforts of modern society. Feeling like she and Harry might have something special, Meghan agreed to spend a week with Harry in the bush. She departed from her friends and met Harry so they could fly to Botswana together.

The time roughing it and doing volunteer work in Africa allowed Harry and Meghan to form an intimate bond. It was a great opportunity for them to really get to know one another without the distractions of work, royal responsibilities, and technology. By the end of their time in Botswana, they had decided to make their relationship official. Meghan had to return to Toronto for the next season of *Suits*, while Harry went back to England. His schedule tended to be much denser than hers, so they agreed that she would fly to the UK whenever she got a chance in order to see him. Occasionally, he would meet her in Canada, and they had a rule that they could not go more than two weeks without seeing each other in person.

Miraculously, Harry and Meghan managed to keep their relationship a secret from the public for several months, allowing them to foster their growing affection without interference. But in November 2016, the fact that they were dating was leaked to the press, forcing Harry to have his communications director release an official statement on the matter. Meghan was slammed by a deluge of negative attention, and many of the rumors and false statements about her caused Harry a great deal of concern. It reminded him so much of the way his mother had been treated by the media, and he was loath to watch another important woman in his life suffer the same treatment.

The couple made their first public appearance together in Toronto during the Invictus Games taking place in September of 2017. As their relationship became stronger, the media's coverage of Meghan took on racist undertones. Several news outlets declared that she was "Straight Outta Compton," referencing the gangsta rap album and song of the same name released by rap group NWA in 1988. This was due to Meghan being half-black, and while she had lived in LA growing up, her homes were nowhere near Compton. The tendency for the press and the public to focus so obsessively on Meghan's race exposed a disconcerting fact about British culture: while there was a veneer of support for minorities, the bulk of society still considered non-white individuals to be inferior.

Great Britain's issues with racism were exacerbated by the push for the referendum on continued European Union (EU) membership in 2016. The Conservative government under Prime Minister David Cameron had vowed to hold a vote on the matter if reelected, and after a successful bid, the vote went forward. This resulted in 51.9% of voters opting for the United Kingdom to pull out of the EU, and Cameron subsequently resigned as prime minister. Theresa May was chosen to succeed him, but the matter of "Brexit," as Britain's exit from the EU was popularly known, would rumble on for nearly half a decade before being settled.

One of the chief issues the citizenry had that caused them to support Brexit was immigration. Just like the people in the United States under President Trump, the United Kingdom saw a rise in nationalism and even white supremacy. It was believed that native citizens and white people, in general, were losing ground to other races, resulting in something of a racial panic. This was embodied in the public's mind by Meghan, who was often depicted as a black foreigner pushing her way into the Royal Family. While many minorities were happy that Meghan's relationship with Harry could indicate that times were changing, the response of the media and general public proved that this was not the case.

The Sun ran a story in November of 2016, not long after the "Straight Outta Compton" headline, where they claimed Meghan had clips of herself on a pornographic website. When it later turned out that someone had merely uploaded clips of her scenes in the TV series Suits that contained no nudity whatsoever, the tabloid was compelled to apologize, although it took them until February 2017 to do so.

It is unknown who was behind the uploads, but some have suggested employees of *The Sun* were the ones responsible, using the ability for anyone to upload videos on the website as a loophole in which they could legally state that Meghan was on the site without fear of recrimination. The fact that this occurred so soon after the press had been criticized for the racist headline seems too coincidental to have not been a deliberate attempt to get back at Meghan.

On November 27th, 2017, Charles announced that Harry and Meghan had gotten engaged. Prior to the proposal, Harry had to receive permission to marry Meghan from his grandmother, as it was required by those in line for the throne to ask for the reigning monarch's approval before they could get married. The period following the announcement of the engagement saw a firestorm of media attention focused on the couple, and much of what was released in the press was incredibly ungenerous to Harry's future wife. The racist articles and social media posts ramped up, becoming more overt in their surface-level criticisms of Meghan. Most of what was said in the media and by the public usually boiled down to calling her a gold digger, attention seeker, and manipulative opportunist. These comments were usually peppered with slurs and phrases that carried racist implications.

In the run-up to the wedding, two members of Meghan's family saw an avenue to gain their own fifteen minutes of fame. Her father, Thomas, was approached by various tabloid publications and paid to stage photos and give them information that they could publish as being from a source "very close to Ms. Markle." Very little of what Thomas told the press was true, but many of the outlets were able to avoid being accused of libel or defamation of character since the things they published technically came from an independent source. The laws preventing journalists from being compelled to reveal the identity of a source also aided them in being able to legally print the false information. Meghan had no idea that her father had been doing this, and it was announced that Thomas would be walking the bride down the aisle during the wedding.

The other member of Meghan's family that used the media to smear her was her older half-sister, Samantha Markle. Publications were ecstatic every time Samantha opened her mouth, as nearly everything she said carried with it a new, scandalous bombshell. In order to boost her own credibility, Samantha claimed to have been very close with Meghan during her childhood and even stated that she had raised Meghan herself for many years. This was patently untrue, and there existed more than enough evidence to debunk the negative statements offered by Samantha, but she didn't let up. Because Samantha didn't conceal her identity as the person behind the quotes as her father did, she could have faced legal consequences, but for the sake of their shared bloodline, Meghan chose to simply issue corrections to the statements instead.

Samantha's own daughter, Ashleigh Hale, verified that her mother's claims were false and made in bad faith. She suggested that Samantha was bitterly envious of Meghan's many successes, with her jealousy growing each time Meghan was mentioned in the media. The engagement to a member of the British Royal Family appeared to have finally set Samantha off, and she erupted in a slew of negativity, spewing untrue statements to anyone willing to listen. After a nasty fight with Samantha, Ashleigh and her mother became estranged. In a display of unmitigated gall, after the invitations to the wedding were sent out, Samantha complained about not receiving one. It was clear that she was both extremely entitled and delusional, as it was absurd that she would think she'd be invited to Meghan's wedding after bashing her in the press for months on end.

Another controversy occurred during Christmas of 2017, when Princess Michael of Kent, a tangential member of the Royal Family without a peerage, chose to wear a blackamoor brooch to a luncheon that day thrown by Elizabeth. The brooch was a caricature of an African man in a submissive pose, which appeared to be similar to other depictions of enslaved Africans. When a photograph of her wearing the brooch was made public, there were some people called it out as being racist. Although Princess Michael insisted that she had no idea that the brooch in the shape of a black man was inappropriate to wear, it's unlikely that all of her assistants and handlers didn't caution her that the brooch might be interpreted as a deliberate offense toward Meghan.

The blackamoor brooch incident was far from the first time Princess Michael had been accused of racism. In 2004, she exchanged racist words with diners in a New York City restaurant. When Harry was embroiled in the controversy over wearing a Nazi uniform, she put out a statement claiming that the British people were "excited" over it in a way that they would not have been having he worn a "hammer and sickle." During a conversation with a phony sheik trying to scam money out of her in 2005, Princess Michael repeatedly insulted the late Princess Diana, calling her a bitter and nasty woman who was jealous of Princess Michael's popularity. She also claimed that Charles only married Diana to have a "womb." Those comments did nothing to endear her to Harry, who was convinced that she had worn the blackamoor brooch specifically to target Meghan with an insult, just like she did with his mother.

With only a few days left before the ceremony was to occur, Meghan got word that a story was about to run in the press exposing her father for taking money in exchange for the staged photos and access to insider information about the wedding. When she tried to contact him, he refused to answer, and the next day, he claimed to the media that he'd had a heart attack and been in the hospital. Desperately trying to reach Thomas to find out what was going on, Meghan sent him numerous text messages and attempted to call him over and over to no avail. When he finally responded, she received a strange series of texts that took a passive-aggressive tone, implying that Meghan didn't care about him and that she and Harry would be happier if he died before the wedding. This seemed suspicious to Meghan, as the way the messages were written didn't match up with how Thomas normally wrote, but when she confronted whoever was behind the texts with this accusation, she was stonewalled. Ultimately, the decision was made to rescind Thomas' invitation, as his presence would only stir up more drama.

While preparing for the wedding, Meghan converted from Protestantism to Anglicanism, receiving baptism and confirmation into the Church of England from Justin Welby, the Archbishop of Canterbury. They held a private ceremony in the Chapel Royal of St James's Palace, using water that came from the River Jordan. This was necessary in order for Meghan to be allowed to marry into the Royal Family since the highest-ranking members were required to be Anglicans, as the ruling monarch was the head of the Church of England. After officially converting to Anglicanism, Meghan became the second divorcee to marry an immediate family member of the current king or queen, following Wallis Simpson.

The wedding of Harry and Meghan took place on May 19th, 2018, at St George's Chapel in Windsor. This was the same chapel where Queen Victoria's eldest son, King Edward VII, had gotten married. Both Harry and William, who was serving as his best man, wore their uniforms from the Blues and Royals regiment. The wedding was broadcast on television across the world, and there were an estimated 27.7 million viewers in the United Kingdom, 23 million viewers in the United States, and hundreds of thousands of viewers globally. As one would expect, this was not as large an audience as the wedding of William and Kate, whose viewership broke records when it aired on television and streamed on the video-sharing website YouTube.

Upon the occasion of their marriage, Elizabeth invested Harry and Meghan as the Duke and Duchess of Sussex, granting them an elevated title as she had done for her son and elder grandson. William and Kate's third child, Prince Louis, was born only 26 days before the wedding, on April 23rd, 2018. Now that his brother had three children who were above Harry in the line of succession, bumping him down to sixth in line, it was just about guaranteed that his title of duke was the highest position within the Royal Family that he would ever receive. With his marriage and extensive charity work, it was time for Harry to step out of William's shadow and become his own man.

CHAPTER 5

The Crownless Prince

The marriage of Harry and Meghan brought with it a brief moment of respite for the couple when it came to the media. They weren't exactly left alone, but the coverage of their activities had started to take on a positive spin. Meghan was lauded as a new kind of royal, bringing a sense of progressivism and modern sensibilities to the Institution. Many people had been critical of the Royal Family in the past over their insistent clinging to outdated traditions and values. Harry and Meghan were seen as being intimately in touch with contemporary society, even more so than William and Kate. However, the complementary nature of the Sussexes in the press created new problems, as they had begun to negatively compare Kate to Meghan.

While Harry and Meghan's popularity soared, the previously "it" couple of the Royal Family, the

Cambridges, saw their own positive reputation slowly erode. This ignited bad feelings between the brothers and their spouses, but they all tried to put the tensions aside and work together on various projects. They continued to make public appearances together, doing their best to prevent their growing issues from leaking to the media. The press picked up on this tension anyway, and a number of articles took note of the fact that there appeared to be some bad blood between Meghan and Kate. Once more, the tabloids were being filled to the brim with rumors and gossip about catfights and deliberate slights between the two women.

Meghan's first public appearance following the wedding came on March 22nd, 2018, when she and Harry attended a garden party that was held to honor Charles' charity work. In July of that year, the couple traveled to Dublin, Ireland, touring the city and meeting with a group of the country's up-and-coming leaders. They were received quite warmly by the local populace, and the visit was considered a great success. The publicity tour continued when Harry and Meghan flew to Sydney, Australia for the 2018 Invictus Games. Again, they were given a warm welcome by the people of Sydney, and there was even more, to celebrate when it was announced that Meghan was pregnant with their first child.

Harry and his wife made stops in Fiji, New Zealand, and Tonga, touring many of the countries in the Pacific Ocean. Their trip lasted 18 days, and they enmeshed themselves in the local cultures. While in New Zealand, the couple dressed in traditional Maori cloaks and exchanged the traditional greeting known as "hongi" with well-wishers who came out to see them. When Harry and Meghan traveled to Wellington, they gave speeches in support of a greater awareness of mental health, which was a cause close to both of their hearts. Meghan also spoke at a ceremony that marked the 125th anniversary of Australian women being given the right to vote.

The next stop for the Sussexes was in Tonga, where they represented Elizabeth at the celebration dedicated to the initiative known as the Queen's Commonwealth Canopy, which sought to preserve the indigenous forests and woodlands so that they could be enjoyed by future generations. Harry and Meghan also got a chance to meet with the king and queen of Tonga for a private conversation. The couple's final stop was in Fiji for the unveiling of a memorial that honored Sergeant Talaiasi Labalaba, a British-Fijian soldier who held off 250 insurgents alone during a 1972 military operation in Oman. Before departing for England, Meghan gave an address at the University of the South Pacific, espousing the opinion that better education for girls and women was the key to encouraging social and economic growth.

After returning home and settling down, the Sussexes resided at Nottingham Cottage, which was located on the grounds of London's Kensington Palace. William and Kate had lived there following their wedding as well, but in 2017 made a move into Kensington Palace itself. Having the two couples so close in proximity to each other didn't help when it came to the media's speculation about the souring relationship between the Duchesses of Sussex and Cambridge. The paparazzi kept a close watch on the palace, using a lack of constant contact between them as evidence that they were feuding. As time went on and Meghan made a few faux pas in her choices of outfits and royal etiquette, the public began to turn on her again.

While Kate had grown up in England's high society, allowing her to quickly adapt to the protocols required of members of the Royal Family, Meghan was at a serious disadvantage. She came from modest roots in the United States, where customs were quite different from those in Great Britain. There were no classes on how to behave like a princess—anyone who married into the family was essentially thrown into the deep end without any swimming lessons. Most royal spouses had at least some experience with that world, such as Diana already being part of the nobility prior to marrying Charles, or Sarah Ferguson, Duchess of York, whose father was a military officer that worked closely with Elizabeth's husband, Prince Philip, as well as his son Charles, long before her marriage to Andrew, Duke of York.

An anonymous palace insider alleged that Harry and William got into a vicious fight one day over their respective wives. Kate was supposedly upset that, from her perspective, it seemed like Meghan was attempting to overshadow her during their public appearances together. She was especially upset that she was being depicted as a stuffy, out-of-touch royal, more like Camilla than Diana. In contrast, Meghan was the cool, stylish royal that Kate had previously been viewed as before she became Harry's wife. William apparently asked his brother to tell Meghan to "tone it down" during public appearances. Harry found this incredibly insulting, considering the amount of negative press heaped on Meghan when she first started dating him.

There were other issues that caused problems between the brothers. Harry was not shy when it came to criticizing the outdated concepts and views held by the Institution, and William took it as a personal attack, considering he was inextricably linked to it as the second heir to the throne and future monarch. When Harry brought up the bullying and abuse Meghan suffered in the media, William insisted that every woman who married into the Royal Family had to go through a period of harsh public scrutiny, as it was basically a rite of passage. He claimed that if Harry and Meghan just kept their heads down and toed the line, it would eventually pass. Harry shot back that it was absurd to allow his wife to go through that and accused William of being no better than the people spouting the abuse.

The combined public appearances of the two couples became less frequent, and they were only seen together when they were in larger groups with other members of the Royal Family. There was an increase in criticism of Meghan, and insider information that painted her in a bad light became more frequent. During an outing where she wore a brown hat with a spiral design, there was a slew of reactions that compared it to the "poop" emoji. While many of these comments merely left it at the comparison or pictures editing the emoji onto her head, there were some concerning posts and tweets that took the opportunity to disparage her as looking like the emoji herself due to the darker color of her skin.

Another point of contention between the two royal couples was the amount of activism undertaken by Harry and Meghan. In some of their volunteering, charity work, and public speeches, they engaged in several political issues. While members of the Royal Family weren't barred from involving themselves in politics, it was frowned upon, particularly by the government. It was expected that the royals would not express any opinions that might be in opposition to their current laws and policies, but the Sussexes showed public support for issues that were sometimes in conflict with the government. However, they refused to be silenced, continuing to push causes that they believed in.

A minor but amusing incident took place in late January 2019 when Harry dropped his smartphone behind a couch at Buckingham Palace. He was unable to reach it, as it had fallen down a narrow slit between the wall and the floor. Several attendants tried to reach the phone to no avail. When it became clear that the couch would need to be moved in order to retrieve the phone, Harry considered just buying a new one. In order to move the couch, he needed to first get permission from the Crown Estate. Due to the fact that the reigning monarch doesn't own Buckingham Palace but is merely occupied by her and held in trust by the Crown Estate, any alterations to the protected contents of the palace had to be signed off on through an officially filed request. Harry was forced to fill out the paperwork and submit it to Robin Francis Budenberg, the chief executive and first commissioner of the Crown Estate.

By the time everything was filed and signed by Budenberg, he then had to bring the documents to Elizabeth for final approval. Obviously, she approved the filing, and Harry was permitted to move the couch for the purpose of retrieving his phone. All he had to do was pull it out slightly from against the wall, and he was able to grab the phone from the recess into which it had fallen. Once he was done, he pushed the couch back against the wall, the entire process taking nearly two hours. The absurdity of the situation was illustrated when Elizabeth popped her head into the room and asked Harry if he managed to get his phone back—she was literally three rooms away from the prince, but protocol meant that they had to go through the proper channels, and Budenberg needed to become involved in order to satisfy the regulations in place. Harry later used this anecdote to describe the inefficiency of the Institution and its outdated policies.

Harry and Meghan went overseas again in February of 2019, this time going to Morocco for three days in Elizabeth's stead. Special medical provisions had to be made for Meghan, who was in her third trimester of pregnancy. The couple stayed together at the palace of King Mohammed VI in a private apartment. Their first stop was a visit to a boarding house for girls, where they spoke about the importance of girls and young women in rural areas receiving the same quality of education as boys. They similarly expressed their support for the empowerment of women, education for girls, a greater degree of inclusivity, and more social entrepreneurship.

On May 6th, 2019, Meghan gave birth to her and Harry's first child, Archie Harrison Mountbatten-Windsor, who became the seventh in line to the throne. The couple was overjoyed by the arrival of their son, and he quickly became the center of their world. Harry was intent on giving Archie everything he didn't have as a child, including a normal life. This presented a problem, though, as it was a policy of the Institution to grant the press access to members of the Royal Family, no matter their age. The Sussexes did their best to shield their son from the media, and it was becoming apparent that they would not be successful in keeping Archie away from public scrutiny while they remained entrenched within the gravitational pull of the monarchy.

Behind the scenes, Harry and Meghan began drawing up plans for their future. They made the decision to separate their public relations officials from those of the Royal Family, breaking with tradition by maintaining an independent office. They continued with their grueling schedule of royal appearances and charity work, but the couple was becoming exhausted. Meghan, in particular, was suffering from mental health issues, feeling depressed and anxious every time the pair went out in public. Social media and the press were making digs at her constantly, chipping away at her self-esteem and self-worth. She would often break down before official functions, but she and Harry had to keep up appearances so as not to tarnish the reputation of the Royal Family.

Relations between the couples didn't improve when the Sussexes purchased Frogmore Cottage, a property that was part of Home Park in Windsor, England. They left Nottingham Cottage, meaning they were no longer on the same grounds as William and Kate. Some interpreted the move as an attempt to put some distance between the couples, while others felt it was an attempt to position themselves closer to the queen, who had moved with Philip to Windsor Castle, which was directly beside Home Park. With the COVID-19 pandemic ramping up across the world, Elizabeth and Philip chose Windsor Castle as their "bubble," and those around them were some of the only people permitted to have access to the queen. There were suggestions that the move to Frogmore Cottage was an attempt to get into the bubble and have more influence with Elizabeth than William and Kate, who remained in Kensington Palace.

The tensions between Meghan and Kate increased during this period. As everyone in the Royal Family garnered criticism for their usage of private jets to travel around the world, significantly increasing their carbon footprint while espousing environmental conservationist opinions, both women found themselves the target of a nasty discourse aimed at them personally. Rumors started bubbling to the surface about problems within the Cambridges' marriage, including accusations of cheating. There was also gossip surrounding the way Kate treated her employees, with several claiming she was a terror as a boss, abusing those beneath her and adopting a very entitled attitude.

On Meghan's end, the public comments about her weren't much kinder than what Kate was receiving. No matter what she did to try to assimilate into the Institution, she was still viewed and treated as an outsider who was intruding on the Royal Family and their long-standing traditions. Her American background as someone of mixed race with a career as an actress and activist made her a constant target with plenty of "faults" that the public zeroed in on. The uncomfortable amount of racism directed at her was also still occurring, despite the tepid attempts by officials representing the Royal Family to bring them to a halt.

The public's disdain for Meghan took a dangerous turn when she received a letter in the mail that contained a racist tirade against her, as well as a white powdery substance that was believed to be anthrax but was later identified as a harmless substance used to simulate anthrax. The letter had been sent to St James's Palace and was addressed to her, but she was not the one who opened it, as it was a policy that any suspicious correspondence would be inspected by professional security officers before being passed along to the royals. A counterterrorism investigation was triggered by the letter, and Scotland Yard became involved since its contents made it a potential racist hate crime. The authorities traced the letter back to its source, but no charges were filed, or arrests made over the matter.

Watching his wife being forced to plaster a smile on her face and wave to the crowds as if there was nothing wrong ate away at Harry. This was the same exact situation that his mother had found herself in around three decades prior. Aware that the pressure of these expectations had been a major factor in his parent's divorce, Harry resolved to take steps that would ensure he and Meghan would not end up going down that same path. It was necessary for the survival of their relationship to take a step back from their royal duties. On January 8th of 2020, the Sussexes' representatives made the announcement that they would no longer serve as senior royals full-time, and they intended to split their time between the United Kingdom and the United States.

The announcement came as a shock to many, and the media dubbed the ensuing controversy "Megxit," playing off the name Brexit, which had been coined during the controversial referendum in 2016. Even the Royal Family was blindsided by it, which didn't help the deteriorating relationship between the various members of the Institution. Harry and Meghan met with the other senior royals on January 13th, 2020, which came to be known as the Sandringham Summit. Five days later, palace officials speaking on behalf of the Royal Family issued a public statement that outlined the agreement between the Sussexes and Elizabeth: Harry and Meghan would no longer serve as working members of the Royal Family, and they would stop using their styles as His and Her Royal Highness. They would remain the Duke and Duchess of Sussex, but their children could not inherit any of their parents' titles.

The Institution decreed that Harry and Meghan would have a year in which they could change their minds and return to the fold, gaining back their lost titles and position within the Royal Family. While they appeared to be adamant in their resolve to remain separated from the Royal Family, certain palace insiders believed that after four or five months of being adrift and on their own, the Sussexes would realize they'd made a mistake and come crawling back. Sources closer to Harry and Meghan expressed the opposite opinion, feeling that once they were free from the strict policies and controlling actions of the Royal Family, they would thrive as an independent and unaffiliated couple.

Plans for Harry and Meghan's exit seemed to change at some point between the announcement that they were leaving and when it actually happened. While it was originally understood that the couple would step back but still retain a limited connection to the monarchy, it was decided that they would make a clean break instead. The Sussexes intended to move to a new home in Canada, where they would still be in a country that was part of the Commonwealth, living there for six months and then spending the other six months at Frogmore Cottage. However, when the finalized agreement for the Sussexes was made public, it contained some very different stipulations than the public had been told earlier and gave a deadline for its completion as the spring of 2020. It stated:

- Harry and Meghan would no longer serve as representatives for the queen, despite earlier statements that they were going to continue to make occasional appearances in her stead.

- The couple will technically keep the style of "His and Her Royal Highness" but won't use it in practice. Instead of using the titles of prince and princess, they would simply be known as Harry, Duke of Sussex, and Meghan, Duchess of Sussex.

- They won't continue to draw money from the British taxpayers and the exchequer, becoming financially independent, and repaying the £2.4 million spent on renovations on Frogmore Cottage.

- Harry would no longer carry out his duties with any branch of the British military and lost the right to serve as an official representative of the Royal Family at any military engagements.

- Rather than the 50/50 split between England and Canada, the Sussexes will remain in North America for the majority of the year.

- Frogmore Cottage would remain their home in Great Britain, but they will be required to pay rent to keep it.

- They were permitted to keep their private patronages and associations, such as with the Invictus Games, but they would lose those associated with the Royal Family itself, like their roles as Commonwealth Youth Ambassadors.

- Charles would continue to aid the couple financially through his private revenue sources.

At the time this plan was released to the public, it was unclear whether the Sussexes would continue to have their personal security agents provided to them by the Royal Family or if they would have to make arrangements for private security agents themselves. It didn't help that palace insiders were leaking conflicting information, with some claiming the crown would continue to pay for their security, and others asserted that their security would be pulled immediately, leaving them open to potential harm. Elizabeth's only comment on the matter didn't help clear things up, as she said, "There are well-established independent processes to determine the need for publicly-funded security."

This was concerning to many people who supported Harry and Meghan, considering the fact that she had been receiving an increase in the number of death threats aimed at her. Pulling their security could leave them vulnerable while they arranged for private protection. Actor, director, and producer Tyler Perry ended up loaning the couple his own private security agents in the interim and even extended an offer for them to stay at one of his many homes, this one in Los Angeles. They were very grateful for the offer and decided to move there instead of Canada upon leaving England for North America.

After everything that Harry and Meghan went through during their departure from the Royal Family, it was clear that the relationship between them and the rest of the Royal Family was very rocky. They made their final public appearance in Great Britain at Westminster Abbey on March 9th of 2020, for the Commonwealth Day service. As expected, the public was not kind to the Sussexes, expressing anger and more racist comments directed at Meghan. On

March 31st, they officially severed ties with the Royal Family and made their exit from the United Kingdom, ready to begin their new life with their son Archie in the United States.

CHAPTER 6

A Royal No More

Although the transition from being a member of the Royal Family to become a private citizen was not easy, it came as a relief to Harry and Meghan. They were now free to focus all their energy on securing new revenue streams and charitable causes close to their hearts rather than having to spend their time attending royal functions to represent the queen. In January 2020, they arrived in Victoria, British Columbia, Canada, where they began renting a house. Around the same time, it was announced that Meghan had signed a deal with Disney to provide voiceovers for future projects. This was the first indication that the Sussexes intended to branch out into other industries than they had previously been permitted to engage in.

Harry and Meghan had security agents protecting them that was provided by the Canadian government until the day that they officially stepped down as members of the Royal Family. Following their transition to private citizens on March 31st, 2020, the security detail was pulled, and the Sussexes began to seek out new accommodations for their small family. When the offer from Tyler Perry was made, they leaped at the chance to move to Los Angeles, where Meghan had grown up. She still had family there, particularly her mother, Doria, which meant that Archie would have the opportunity to see his maternal grandmother on a more regular basis.

After their time in Tyler Perry's LA home, the couple decided to abandon their plans to return to Canada and opted to settle permanently in LA instead. In the spring of 2020, as they were still staying at Perry's residence, President Trump tried to piggyback off the controversy of Megxit by making unprompted declarations that the United States would not fund any security detail for the couple. In response, they stated that they never asked for it, nor would they have expected the American people to pay for their safety. The couple searched for a new house during the spring and summer of that year.

On April 6th, 2020, Harry and Meghan established a non-profit organization named Archewell, named after their son Archie. According to their website, the name was also chosen due to the Greek root of the word "arche," which means "a source of action," and "well," which they define as "a plentiful source or supply; a place we go to dig deep." They intended to direct many of their charity efforts through this new organization, which would allow them greater control over ensuring any funds raised for a cause reached the proper recipients. The Archewell Foundation and Archewell Fund were both formed to function as different subsidiaries of the organization.

Fourteen days later, the couple released a statement clarifying that they would no longer be cooperating with the British press, particularly the tabloids like the Daily Mirror, the *Daily Mail, the Daily Express*, and *The Sun*. This was in defiance of the expectations by the press that they are given access to every member of the Royal Family. Now that the Sussexes had ceased to be an official part of the Institution, they had no incentive to continue adhering to the invasive policies that prevented them from enjoying a private life without fear that everything they did could potentially end up in the tabloids. The statement was made more for the principle of the matter since the press had been eviscerating the couple since the moment, they revealed their plans to step back from the Royal Family, and affirming their intention to deny exclusive access to their lives had no appreciable effect on the negative content generated by the media.

In July 2020, Harry and Meghan purchased a mansion located in Montecito, California, and moved from Perry's home to their new residence. Two months later, they repaid the full amount of £2.4 million for the refurbishments of Frogmore House to the taxpayers of Great Britain. Although part of the agreement with the Royal Family when they decided to leave was that Charles would pay to help support them for a year as they settled into their new lives, he withdrew monetary assistance soon after their move to North America. Fortunately, Diana had left Harry £6.5 million that had been invested before her death and accrued interest over the years. By the time Harry turned 30 years old, there was more than £10 million in the portfolio.

The 2020 London Marathon was originally set to be held in April and would have been one of the first major appearances made by the Sussexes since severing ties with the Royal Family, but the event had to be postponed until October 2020 due to concerns over COVID-19. Similarly, the Invictus Games had been scheduled for May but was pushed back to October 2021. Confined to their home due to COVID-19 restrictions, the couple allowed Harry's cousin, Princess Eugenie, and her husband, Jack Brooksbank, to live at Frogmore for a period of six weeks. Eugenie and Jack were previously confined to her parent's home but sought somewhere they could have more privacy. However, the proximity to the queen's own residence brought with it the same intrusions from paparazzi as Harry and Meghan had experienced while living there, causing the young couple to seek a residence with more privacy to dwell.

Following the holidays, which Harry, Meghan, and Archie spent in isolation at their mansion in Montecito, the slowly loosening pandemic restrictions allowed people to travel and work under specific conditions and precautions. On March 7th, 2021, a bombshell interview conducted by media mogul and television host Oprah Winfrey with the Duke and Duchess of Sussex aired nationwide in the United States on CBS and was rebroadcasted the next day in the United Kingdom on ITV. The interview covered many of the topics concerning Harry and Meghan's relationship, from its inception to the present day, and revealed many of the behind-the-scenes details that they had been prevented from divulging while still under the strict rules and policies of the Royal Family.

Early in the interview, Harry and Meghan made a clear distinction between the individual members of the Royal Family and the Royal Family as an Institution. Many of their issues were with the latter, which was basically run like a business due to the massive amount of money it generated every year. "It's hard for people to distinguish the two because it's a family business, right, there's the family, and then there are the people that are running the institution; those are two separate things," Meghan stated. "The Queen, for example, has always been wonderful to me."

Meghan recalled how poorly she was prepared upon entering life with the Royal Family. She hadn't even been instructed in the proper way to curtsy when meeting the queen, only learning about it from the Duchess of York minutes ahead of her first introduction to Elizabeth, practicing right outside the Royal Lodge before entering. Much of her first few years in a relationship with Harry was like "on the job" training, figuring out what to do and how to do it by trial and error. This was very frustrating to her because the women of the Royal Family had very specific expectations of the way they would dress and behave in public, but since Harry was a man and didn't have much experience in that area, he wasn't aware of everything she needed to do.

Part of the problem when it came to the way Meghan presented herself to the outside world was that she knew almost nothing about what it meant to be a royal, having paid very little attention to the Institution of the British monarchy while growing up and living in America. She was only vaguely aware of their activities, and most of it was confined to the charity and volunteer work performed by Diana when she was still alive. Meghan had assumed it would be more like the United States presidency, where people expected them to carry themselves with a bit more dignity and politeness to members of the general public but nothing too far outside the experience of the average citizen.

Instead, there were rules she had never even considered before, such as how women in the Royal Family could not wear the same style or color of clothing as the queen and also needed to wear something different from anyone with a more senior position. However, the queen and senior royals never relayed what outfits they would be wearing on any given day, so Meghan basically had to just guess and hope for the best. This led her to restrict her fashion choices to colors and styles that the other women never wore, which translated to mostly neutral-tone outfits, like white, beige, or tan. This made it hurt a bit more when her fashion style was criticized in the British press since she wasn't actually allowed to wear what she wanted, but nobody knew of that fact.

There was also some suspicion that jealousy played a role in the way Meghan was treated by the Royal Family. Despite the significant amount of racism directed her way right from the start of her relationship with Harry, her presence was still considered to be a "breath of fresh air." She provided a much-needed progressive voice near the throne, as some of the younger members of the Royal Family felt upset at the implication that they were lesser in the eyes of the people. Because of this, they didn't offer as much aid or support to Meghan as they could have, secretly hoping to see her constantly fail to adhere to expectations, eroding her initial surge of popularity.

Another issue Meghan took with the way the Royal Family operated was how they often were aware of the truth when false claims were put out by the media but rarely did anything to correct them when it involved her. Around the time of Harry and Meghan's wedding, the press put out a story wherein they accused Meghan of having made Kate cry while preparing for the ceremony. However, the truth was that it had been Kate who made Meghan cry over a problem with the flower girl dresses. While the pair made up soon after, and Kate had sent her a note with some flowers as an apology, palace officials never bothered to issue a correction to the erroneous story, leaving the general public under the impression that she'd been a "bridezilla."

The Royal Family made it very clear to Meghan early on that she was not permitted to speak to the media on her own behalf, and everything she wished to say needed to go through the palace press office. But the Sussexes did not have their own representative, instead sharing one with more senior members of the Royal Family. This meant that in any situation where there was a conflict of interest, the officials always made sure anything released helped the higher-ranking royals at her and Harry's expense. Even when people were posting or publishing absolutely heinous lies about Meghan, she could not make a statement to defend herself. It also seemed like on the few occasions when the officials did speak up on her behalf; they took their time in getting anything done. A prime example was the claim that she had videos on a pornographic website. This was seriously damaging to her reputation, yet it took them over three months to correct the matter.

Meghan naïvely believed that if she played by their rules, at the very least, she would be protected by them in return. This turned out not to be the case. When Archie was born, she and Harry were informed that he would not be granted any titles, which meant he was not entitled to have a security detail. The Sussexes were very upset by this, but Harry was especially incensed. He didn't care about the title, but he was intimately familiar with how imperative it was for a child within the upper level of the Royal Family to have official protection. When he started school as a boy, the media were ruthless in doing anything possible to capture candid photos of him, invading his privacy and making him feel unsafe. However, he had been protected by security agents, who often stopped the most egregious offenders without him knowing about it at the time. Security was a major sticking point for Harry since he saw what could happen to a member of the Royal Family when they weren't properly protected. It made him think of his mother, and he had no desire to risk his own child's life.

Harry and Meghan also feared that leaving Archie exposed could be more dangerous than if he had been William and Kate's son. The racist tone of the criticism against Meghan being mixed race had already spread to their son, who was also mixed race. Harry revealed a galling conversation he had with another member of the Royal Family, where they expressed concern over how dark Archie's skin might be when compared to the other royals. This made him realize that there would never be any protection for his wife and child against such regressive attitudes since people within his own family held similar beliefs. Although he refused to name which member of the Royal Family this conversation occurred with, most of the speculation concurs that it was either Philip or Charles.

There were some bad feelings between the Sussexes and the Royal Family stemming from the allegations of sexual misconduct by Prince Andrew that picked up traction near the end of 2019. Rumors had persisted for years that Andrew maintained a relationship with convicted sex offender Jeffrey Epstein, the first of which dates all the way back to 2011. When Virginia Giuffre accused Epstein of having paid her $15,000 to sleep with Andrew when she was still underage, the Royal Family expressed support for the Duke of York. When he later settled a lawsuit with her out of court, his mother, Elizabeth, and brother Charles were said to have helped him pay it out of their own pockets.

In November 2019, the BBC program *Newsnight* conducted an interview with Andrew that had been approved by the queen. However, the things he told journalist Emily Maitlis that were supposedly meant to defend himself only made things worse. The public was outraged following its broadcast, especially in how nonchalantly he recounted visiting Epstein, even after Epstein's conviction for sexual assault against a minor. Andrew was heard calling Epstein's home "a convenient place to stay" and insisted he did not regret his relationship with the convicted sex offender, as it had been useful to him over the years. The assertion near the end of the interview that Andrew's most recent visit to Epstein was solely for the purpose of ending their personal relationship came off as pretty hollow.

Following the outrageous interview, Andrew appeared to be in complete denial of reality when he was quoted as saying he was pleased with how the whole thing turned out. However, the rest of the public erupted in outrage after seeing how arrogant and without remorse Andrew behaved. The Royal Family had spent years covering for him because he played his role without complaint, but the interview made the whole mess far too difficult to sweep under the rug again. The queen suspended him from all royal duties, and he was more or less exiled from the Royal Family. What hurts the most for Harry and Meghan after discovering the truth behind Andrew was the fact that the Royal Family bent over backward to protect Andrew from the true allegations of sexual misconduct against a minor but couldn't be bothered to defend Meghan against the racist diatribes of the media.

The Oprah interview brought up another issue that Harry and Meghan had worked to bring awareness to for years: mental health. Meghan revealed that the intense pressure and constant stream of abuse from the public caused her to enter a deep depression, and she was even suicidal at some points. When she sought out palace officials to help check her into a hospital, she was denied the ability to go, as they claimed it would not look good for the Royal Family. All of her important documents, such as her driver's license, passport, and credit cards, had been confiscated by palace officials prior to her wedding under the guise of holding them for safekeeping. Without any of those items, she could not seek out treatment on her own, which only caused her to spiral even deeper into a depressive state.

During this period, Meghan had gotten in touch with one of Diana's best friends. This friend understood what the Duchess of Sussex was going through, noting that Diana herself suffered in a way very similar to Meghan. Harry, too, was concerned about the similarities he was seeing between his wife and late mother. It was around this time that he'd resolved to take a step back from the Royal Family, although he had no idea what form that might take. His primary concern was the health and safety of his wife and child. Everything else was secondary, and the details could be worked out later. Unfortunately, he did not receive very much support from the Royal Family. They took his wish to limit his and Meghan's public appearances and royal duties as a personal insult.

This is why there was so much confusion surrounding the couple's exit. Harry and Meghan had only wanted to ease up on how often they attended official functions, allowing them to have more time to focus on their own mental health and to give the press and public fewer opportunities to criticize Meghan.

However, once the Royal Family was made aware of his intentions, they insisted that if Harry wanted to step back, he had to remove himself completely. There was no room for a middle ground with them. He suspected that this "all or nothing" attitude was a gambit on the Royal Family's part, as they assumed that when faced with this ultimatum, he would relent. Instead, he accepted it, and the palace officials had to rush to construct an exit plan for them.

Although the interview with Oprah did not help with the Sussexes' reputation in the United Kingdom, the revelations brought them more support from elsewhere around the world. Harry knew that the interview would likely alienate him further from his family, but he felt it was too important that his and Meghan's truth be conveyed to the world, especially during a time when so many people were feeling trapped in their lives. Mental health problems, while gaining more awareness in the last few years, are still heavily stigmatized. Meghan had hoped that sharing her own struggles, it would encourage more people to seek out help without feeling shame.

The day after the interview first aired, noted British broadcaster and blowhard Piers Morgan was very vocal in his disdain for Harry and Meghan. The Duchess of Sussex was especially a target of his impotent rage. He ranted for nearly ten minutes straight, his puffy face turning bright crimson before taking on a tinge of blue as if his tirade was preventing enough oxygen from reaching his brain. Morgan had made it a tradition to trash Meghan on his show, and even as he denied the blatant instances of racism, he himself implied on numerous occasions that Meghan was unfit for the role of a royal due to her "background." Morgan went on to prove exactly why people continue to hide their mental health issues when he called Meghan a liar over her revelation that she was struggling with depression and suicidal thoughts.

Although Morgan later apologized after getting raked over the coals, it came off as very disingenuous, and very few people believed he had done so as anything more than damage control. One commenter threw his own words used against Meghan back at him, writing, "I don't believe a word Piers Morgan says. I wouldn't believe him if he read me a weather report." However, when Morgan suffered the consequences of his actions, having an investigation into misconduct opened against him and subsequently being forced to resign from his role as a presenter on *Good Morning Britain*, he immediately proved how much of a two-faced snake he is by rescinding all of his apologies and doubling down on his criticism of Meghan. Ultimately, Morgan shot himself in the foot, exposing himself as a disgusting human being who pushes a racist agenda and mocks people with mental health problems, as well as a coward who won't stand behind his own words when he thinks his bank account might lose a few pounds.

Unlike Morgan, when then-current Prime Minister Boris Johnson was asked about the interview, he made the wise decision and refrained from comment, stating, "When it comes to matters to do with the Royal Family, the right thing for prime ministers to say is nothing." Unfortunately, other members of the Conservative Party couldn't help themselves, feeling the need to respond. Zac Goldsmith, the Minister of State for Foreign Affairs, tweeted, "Harry is blowing up his family. What Meghan wants; Meghan gets." Presumably, he believed Meghan wanted years of being slammed in the press for minor perceived infractions against royal etiquette and racist abuse since that's what she got.

Conversely, Keir Starmer, Leader of the Opposition, opined that Meghan's claims about racism and lack of support for mental health issues should be taken "very, very seriously." Kate Green, the Shadow Secretary of State for Education, called the allegations "shocking" and "really distressing." Diane Abbott, the Shadow Home Secretary, backed up the assertions made during the interview, saying she could point to "story after story when Meghan was treated quite differently from white members of the Royal Family." As a direct result of the interview, a debate in the House of Commons ended with an open letter signed by 72 women in Parliament that were brought before the queen, asking her to seek out solutions to avoid the "hounding" of high-profile women like the Duchess of Sussex by the media.

Harry and Meghan received more support from leaders in other countries than they did in the United Kingdom. President Joe Biden told journalists that he would praise anyone who had the courage to speak up for those suffering from mental health issues, particularly when the current climate in society still looked down on those who did negatively. Canadian Prime Minister Justin Trudeau stated, "I won't comment on what's going on over in the U.K., but I will continue to endeavor to fight against racism and intolerance every single day in Canada." Debbie Ngarewa-Packer, a member of New Zealand's Parliament, criticized the Royal Family's response to the interview and bitterly noted, "I don't know why everyone is so surprised that the Crown is racist."

Despite the revelations from the Oprah interview, life continued on unabated in Great Britain, including almost daily stories painting Harry and Meghan in a negative light. Although the couple had never been treated fairly by the press, the position taken by the media following their departure could be summed up as "if you're not with us, you're against us." The fact their insistence that Harry and Meghan were "ungrateful" for abandoning their position within the Royal Family without a hint of irony, when that very same press drove them away, seemed to be completely lost on those within the British media. It was obvious that, contrary to their claims, the press was not as fair-minded as they liked to believe and refused to admit that they played a major role in causing Harry and Meghan to leave.

Meghan's father, Thomas, reached out to *Good Morning Britain* and appeared on the show's March 9th episode. He publicly apologized to his daughter for taking money from the tabloids and conspiring with them to feed them insider information in the leadup to her wedding. Although he said he understood why Meghan felt betrayed by him and that his actions caused them to become estranged, it came off more like he was merely using the significant amount of attention garnered by the Oprah interview to once again position himself in the spotlight. This viewpoint was strengthened when he hand-delivered a letter to the offices of Oprah Winfrey on March 25th, requesting that she conduct an interview with him about the situation with his daughter. Unsurprisingly, Oprah declined this offer.

The Royal Family itself issued several statements in the wake of the interview, some of which came as a surprise to palace watchers. A March 9th press release said, "The issues raised, particularly that of race, are concerning. While some recollections may vary, they are taken very seriously and will be addressed by the family privately. Harry, Meghan, and Archie will always be much-loved family members." Another source close to the Royal Family said that in order to address the issues raised in the interview, there needed to be a review of "the policies, the procedures, and programs in place," and admitted that "we haven't seen the progress we would like in terms of representation and more needs to be done. We can always improve." They claimed it was still too soon to announce any firm plans concerning this matter but that key members of the Royal Family supported the idea that the royal households should put someone in charge of inclusivity and diversity.

While William was visiting a school in East London on March 11th, he was asked for a comment about the situation. He responded, "We're very much not a racist family." William and Kate's reaction to the Sussexes leaving the Royal Family, as well as the bombshell interview, showed that they were firmly against Harry and Meghan's actions and decisions. By this point, the brothers were barely speaking, and it appeared unlikely that they would be resolving their differences anytime soon. The Duke of

Cambridge was heard privately chastising Harry and Meghan for "making waves," insisting that the criticism in the press was no worse for Meghan than it was for his own wife. It seemed he completely neglected to factor in the reality that even if Kate had received the same amount of abuse, it never attacked her for the color of her skin or her ethnicity.

Gayle King, a presenter on the television program *CBS This Morning,* reported during the March 16th episode that, prior to the Sussexes' decision to step back from the Royal Family, Harry had attempted to broach the topic of racism targeting his wife with both Charles and William. However, his concerns were rebuffed, and it became clear to him that their conversations were unproductive, and Harry was unable to open his family's eyes to what he and Meghan were going through. It should not have come as a surprise when Harry and Meghan withdrew from the Institution, but neither his father nor his brother could have conceived that Harry would actually go through with it.

On April 9th of 2021, Harry's grandfather, Prince Philip, died at the age of 99 years old while residing in Windsor Castle. The only reason given by the Royal

Family for his cause of death was "old age." At the time of his passing, he was the longest-serving consort to a monarch in British history, spending an unprecedented 69 years at his wife Elizabeth's side. The regular funeral ceremony for the public was not able to be held, as COVID-19 restrictions for large gatherings remained in effect. Instead, a private, intimate funeral was held at St George's Chapel in Windsor Castle. He was interred within the Royal Vault at the chapel, although this was meant to only be a temporary arrangement, as he was to be moved to join Elizabeth beneath the King George VI Memorial Chapel, which Elizabeth had commissioned for her late father in 1962.

Officially, Meghan was not invited to the funeral because of the COVID-19 restrictions, but privately, palace insiders admit that the decision on whether she should be allowed to attend would have been much more difficult as the Royal Family's minds were split on the matter. Ultimately, the conundrum was moot, and Harry traveled to the United Kingdom alone. Meghan sent her condolences alongside the representatives from countries all around the world. Philip's last will and testament were read in the presence of his immediate family, but their contents were not released to the public. Some had speculated that it might contain material that could be damaging to the reputation of the Royal Family since when the High Court made the ruling that it was to remain sealed to the public for 90 years, they justified their decision by stating it was to protect the "dignity and standing" of Elizabeth. Whether those documents held anything pertaining to the Sussexes won't be revealed for a very long time.

Amidst the drama stirred up by the Oprah interview and Philip's subsequent death, Meghan's third pregnancy flew under the radar for a time. She had previously been pregnant for a second time in the spring and summer of 2020, right around the time when they purchased the estate of Riven Rock in Montecito. Unfortunately, that August, she suffered from a miscarriage. While it cannot be determined for certain whether the stress, she was under during the couple's withdrawal from the Royal Family contributed to her losing the baby, it absolutely didn't help matters. But the Sussexes were blessed a second time with a child on June 4th, 2021. This time, they had a daughter, who they subsequently named

Lilibet Diana Mountbatten-Windsor. Their new daughter's names were chosen in honor of Elizabeth, who was nicknamed Lilibet in her youth, and Harry's late mother.

Despite the claims of some supposed palace insiders that the queen was insulted that Harry and Meghan had used her old nickname as their daughter's first name, it was later revealed that Harry had actually sought permission to give his child that name. Elizabeth was delighted and honored by their choice and wished both the girl and her family well. Lilibet was given her own nickname by her parents, who lovingly called her "Lili." Archie was thrilled to have a younger sibling, taking his new role as big brother very seriously. In contrast to the other royal children, Lilibet wasn't seen by the public until her first Christmas, when a picture for a Christmas card was released that depicted her with the rest of her family.

Throughout the beginning of 2022, Harry and Meghan continued to operate their charitable endeavors through the Archewell Foundation, as well as patronize the various other organizations that they were allowed to keep their preexisting relationships with upon leaving the Royal Family. The 2021 Invictus

Games have been postponed again, this time until April 2022. The Fifth Annual Invictus Games was held at the Hague in the Netherlands. Harry and Meghan were in attendance, joined by Princess Margriet of the Netherlands, her son, Prince Pieter-Christiaan, and King Willem-Alexander of the Netherlands, the country's ruling monarch. On their way to the Hague, the couple stopped by England to visit Elizabeth and Charles. However, their brief stop in England was not reported on in the media, as the Royal Family wished to keep it quiet.

A month after Philip's funeral, there was a spate of break-ins at Harry and Meghan's California home. Within 12 days, there were multiple trespassers who tripped alarms, and the Santa Barbara Police Department responded to these incidents. The safety of his family was a sore spot for Harry, especially after the Royal Family had withdrawn their security detail, so he was insistent that they beef up their estate's security measures. The Royal Family was aware of numerous threats to the Sussexes' safety, as a representative from the National Police Chiefs' Council's Counter, Terrorism Policing revealed later that year. While they had investigated some of these threats, leading to the prosecution of those responsible, many others were simply ignored.

In June of 2022, Harry and Meghan made their first official trip back to the United Kingdom for Queen Elizabeth II's Platinum Jubilee, celebrating her 70th anniversary as Queen of Great Britain. They attended a Thanksgiving Service on June 3rd that was held at St Paul's Cathedral. The Sussexes didn't stay very long during this visit, but they were scheduled to return in September for charity events in both England and Germany. The couple did indeed travel back to the United Kingdom in September, but it was for a very different reason.

Queen Elizabeth II died on September 8th, 2022, while staying at Balmoral Castle in Scotland. This made her the first British monarch to die in Scotland since King James V of Scotland in 1542. At the time of her death, Elizabeth was 96 years old and had spent 70 years sitting on the throne. As with her husband, the only official cause of death was "old age." She had continued to carry out her duties to the country right up until the end, accepting the resignation of Boris Johnson and the appointment of

Liz Truss as his successor to the position of the prime minister just two days before she passed away.

When it became clear that Elizabeth wasn't long for this world, the closest members of the Royal Family were contacted and told to come to Balmoral with great haste. Charles arrived with Camilla shortly before his mother died, and he and his sister Anne were by her side when she took her last breath. Elizabeth's other children, Prince Andrew and Prince Edward, as well as her elder grandson, Prince William, arrived at the castle a few hours after her death. Edward's wife, Sophie, Countess of Wessex, had accompanied him, but William's wife, Kate, did not. Harry made it to Balmoral last, and like his brother, he did not bring his wife.

Upon the passing of Elizabeth, Charles became the new King of Great Britain. At the age of 73, he broke the record for the oldest person to be crowned king, beating out the previous record holder, King William IV, who was 64 years old when he inherited the throne in 1830. King Charles III, as he was now known, didn't have much time to orient himself before being thrust immediately into his first official duty: bring the body of his mother and predecessor home. His ascension meant that everyone beneath him in the line of succession now moved up a spot—William was the heir presumptive to the throne, his son George was second in line, and his other two children were third and fourth. Harry returned to being fifth in the line of succession, as he had been prior to the birth of William's youngest son.

The late queen's body was sent to Edinburgh for a ceremony put on by the Scottish people to honor Elizabeth, making a number of stops along the way to allow mourners to say their goodbyes. Her funeral procession traveled through Fife, Aberdeen, Dundee, Perth and Kinross, and Angus before it reached the city. In Aberdeenshire, a group of local farmers came out on their tractors and formed a "guard of honor" for the duration of Elizabeth's time within their area. After arriving in Edinburgh, a Thanksgiving service was held to celebrate the queen's life and her connections to Scotland.

On September 13th, Elizabeth's body was flown from Edinburgh to London for her state funeral. Once in London, she was taken to Buckingham Palace in a state hearse and then placed in the Bow Room at the palace in the company of the Royal Family. Later, a military escort led the procession as the queen was brought from the palace to Westminster Hall, where she was scheduled to lay in state for five days until the funeral was held. Honor guards protected the coffin, and members of the public were permitted to walk past it to bid their late queen farewell. It was estimated that around a quarter of a million people filed through Westminster Hall to see Elizabeth one last time.

The late queen's body was moved from Westminster Hall to Westminster Abbey on September 19th. Westminster Abbey was the same place where Elizabeth's coronation had taken place in 1953. Before the service began, the bells of the abbey rang once per minute for 96 minutes straight. Every time the bell rang, it represented a single year in Elizabeth's long life. Charles, William, and other members of the Royal Family who had served in the military wore their dress uniforms to the funeral. Since both Harry and Andrew were considered "non-working" royals, they did not wear their own uniforms.

The funeral service for Elizabeth was conducted by David Michael Hoyle, the Dean of Westminster, using the *Book of Common Prayer* (1662) as a guide. Liz Truss, the newly-appointed prime minister, and Baroness Patricia Scotland, Secretary General of the Commonwealth, both gave readings during the service. There were psalms with music set to them written by British composer Judith Weir, called "Like as the Hart," and one by Scottish composer and conductor James MacMillan, titled "Who Shall Separate Us?" The funeral service ended with the bagpipe lament known as "Sleep, Dearie, Sleep," and Sir Edward William Elgar's *Organ Sonata in G Major* was played while mourners departed from the abbey.

Another procession took place as Elizabeth was carried from London to Windsor. A committal service was held at St George's Chapel, with around 800 guests in attendance. The Dean of Windsor led the committal service, and at the end of it, the Imperial State Crown, scepter, and orb—the three symbols of the monarchy—were taken from the coffin and placed on the altar. As per tradition, the current Lord Chamberlain broke his staff of office in half in a symbolic gesture to represent the end of his service to the queen. The broken halves of the staff were then set atop Elizabeth's coffin. She was lowered into the Royal Vault to bring the service to a close.

Following the committal service, everyone other than Elizabeth's closest family members departed. Those who remained behind had a private service as she was interred beneath the King George VI Memorial Chapel. Elizabeth's father, George VI, had been reinterred there in 1969 after the completion of the chapel, and her mother, Elizabeth, as well as the coffin containing the ashes of her sister Margaret, were all buried beneath the chapel. The remains of Philip, which had sat in the Royal Vault since his death the year before, were brought to the King George VI Memorial Chapel and laid to rest beside his beloved wife and queen.

Interestingly, Elizabeth's coffin had actually been constructed 30 years before her death. She had wanted to ensure that when the time came, the coffin was ready to go. It was constructed from the sturdy wood of an English oak tree, and it was lined with lead to prevent any moisture from seeping in and causing structural damage. Because of this, the coffin was incredibly heavy, requiring no less than eight pallbearers to lift and carry it, as opposed to the standard number of six. The interment area beneath the King George VI Memorial Chapel has room for six coffins. At present, five of those spaces have been filled, leaving room for one more. Presumably, if Charles wishes to be buried with his mother, that space is reserved for him.

Although Charles is now the ruling monarch, his coronation isn't set to take place until May 6th of, 2023. Since it's a state function, the British government is in control of the guest list, meaning only those members of Parliament who extend an invitation will be permitted to attend. While Harry, as one of Charles' only two sons, is expected to receive an invitation, it remains to be seen whether Meghan or their children will be asked to come. Based on the current climate between the Sussexes and the British people, it could go either way. William, Kate, and their children will undoubtedly be present as Charles is officially crowned, and it might serve as a good olive branch if the Royal Family ensures that Harry's family is invited as well.

The future of relations between the Sussexes and the United Kingdom seems to be slowly stabilizing, but that may change quite soon. In early December of

2022, the streaming service Netflix began putting out episodes of a documentary series titled *Harry & Meghan*, which is set to have six episodes in total. In the series, Harry and Meghan discuss much of what has happened to them since the pair got together, and can be seen as something of a supplement to the Oprah Winfrey interview. They appear more at ease on camera, a fact that they ascribe to having more freedom, to tell the truth behind their story, unfettered by the shackles of the Institution and its suffocating policies and regulations. They appear to merely want the world to know their side of the story, especially since so much of what occurred was only filtered through the lens of the Royal Family's public relations apparatus.

Another potential spanner in the works for an amicable reunion between the Duke and Duchess of Sussex and the rest of the Royal Family is the autobiography Spare, which is scheduled to be released in early 2023. Depending on what information Harry has chosen to include in his book, there might only be more bad feelings and angry shouts of betrayal if he exposes any dark secrets still lurking beneath the surface of the monarchy.

However, Harry's number one priority has always been keeping his wife and children safe, no matter who might be trying to harm them. If the Royal Family poses a threat to Meghan, Archie, and Lilibet, there is no doubt that Harry will conjure the warrior from within to protect those he loves.

Conclusion

Prince Harry is an incredibly complex individual. He was raised from birth in a world to which almost nobody else can possibly relate. For most of his life, he was a perennial "backup," only important to the machinery of the Royal Family insofar as he might potentially be needed if tragedy struck, rendering the preferred heirs unable to take the throne. The problem with the line of succession is that nothing in this world is ever guaranteed. What people expect to happen and what actually occurs aren't always the same thing. Was it not for an American actress and divorcee who married into the Royal Family, the shape of the line of succession would have looked very different right now? But this wasn't American actress and divorcee Meghan Markle—it was Wallis Simpson.

Without Edward VIII's decision to marry Wallis and step away from the throne, his younger brother would have never become king. If his brother never became king, Elizabeth would have never become queen. After that, it's entirely likely that the entire course of Elizabeth's life would have changed, and she may never have met Philip and given birth to Charles. No Charles means no Princess Diana and certainly no William or Harry. It's impossible to say whether the United Kingdom would be in a better or worse position than it is right now, but the significant amount of good that has come out of the Royal Family, including the tireless commitment to charity and activism by members like Diana, Harry, and Meghan.

It seems like the British media and general public are still punishing the Royal Family for the "sins" of Edward and Wallis from almost a century ago. They undoubtedly view Meghan as being in the same mold as Wallis Simpson, which is why so much of the discourse surrounding her seems to depend on the assumption that Meghan is manipulating her husband. Wallis endured the exact same accusations when her own husband did the unthinkable, giving up one of the most prestigious positions in the entire world just so that he could be with her. It never occurs to critics that sometimes, there are people who place a greater value on love than power.

Harry is also his own man. If he wanted to remain a full-time member of the Royal Family, that's exactly what he would have done. But he had already gone through the wringer as a child, a teenager, and a young adult. The amount of scrutiny on someone who is always in the public eye can become exhausting and detrimental to their mental health. He saw what it did to his mother, and the abuse she suffered at the hands of the press was disconcertingly echoed in the kinds of things being said about his wife. Nobody should have to experience such an unrelenting barrage of hate, no matter what position they hold within society.

The fact of the matter is that Harry was never given a choice about what he wanted to do with his life. He was the "spare" to his older brother's status as the "heir." Just about everybody else in the world is granted the opportunity to decide their future. If your father is a plumber, you aren't forced to become a plumber and remain a plumber. If your mother chooses to live in Florida, you aren't required to live close by in order to stand in for her when she can't go to the grocery store. Growing up, it was expected that Harry would follow the path laid out for him at the moment of his birth and that he would continue to play by the rules, putting the needs of the Institution before those of himself or his loved ones. The moment he expressed a desire to do something else with his life, the people he'd dutifully served for decades turned on him in the blink of an eye.

Nobody says you have to like Harry or Meghan. You can have whatever opinion you want of them, be it positive or negative. But you must give them the minimum amount of respect that is afforded to everyone else in society. Abuse, bullying, and racism are unacceptable ways to express your opinions. Criticisms can be leveled at a person without reducing them to their skin color, religion, or place of birth. There is never a justifiable reason to harass another person purely because they are more visible than the average citizen. If you can't get your point across without devolving into insults and slurs, then you didn't have anything useful to say in the first place.

Whatever the future may bring for Harry and Meghan, it will at least be something that they are able to choose. It appears that they are quite content at the moment, residing on their estate in California and raising their two children far away from the smothering world of the Royal Family. They are still pushing awareness for causes they believe need more attention and donating much of their time to helping out those who are less fortunate. It looks like Harry found a perfect match in Meghan, and so long as they have each other, whatever problems arise in their lives will be confronted head-on and side by side. He was saddled with the identity of the "spare" at birth, but the world couldn't spare losing such an intelligent, driven, and compassionate soul.

Did you enjoy this book? Consider leaving a review on amazon if you enjoyed this book

References

Bates, S. (2005, September 15). Harry at 21 on Camilla, the media and Aids children in Africa. The Guardian. https://www.theguardian.com/uk/2005/sep/15/monarchy.stephenbates

BBC NEWS. (n.d.). BBC. http://news.bbc.co.uk/2/hi/uk_news/3762200.stm

BBC News. (2018, October 22). Royal tour: Harry and Meghan's overseas trip so far. BBC. https://www.bbc.com/news/in-pictures-45939855

BBC News. (2020, September 7). Prince Harry: Frogmore Cottage renovation cost repaid. BBC. https://www.bbc.com/news/uk-54062799

BBC News. (2022, September 8). King Charles III, the new monarch. BBC. https://www.bbc.com/news/uk-59135132

BBC says sorry to Diana's brother Earl Spencer for interview 'deceit.' (n.d.). Times (London, England:

1788). https://www.thetimes.co.uk/article/bbc-says-sorry-to-dianas-brother-earl-spencer-for-interview-deceit-ghfjqbbbx

Brandreth, G. (2005). Charles and Camilla. Century.

Brown, T. (2022). The Palace Papers: Inside the House of Windsor--the truth and the turmoil. Crown.

Casualties. (n.d.). The-monitor.org. http://www.the-monitor.org/en-gb/reports/2019/landmine-monitor-2019/casualties.aspx

Clinton, J. (2022, December 10). What is a Blackamoor brooch? Controversy around Princess Michael explored in Harry & Meghan, explained. INews. https://inews.co.uk/news/blackamoor-brooch-what-princess-michael-harry-and-meghan-explained-2018258

Dangremond, S. (2017, December 11). A look back at prince Harry's former girlfriends. Town & Country. https://www.townandcountrymag.com/society/g14383928/prince-harry-ex-girlfriends-dating-history-relationships/

Dodd, V. (2018, February 22). White powder letter sent to Meghan Markle treated as racist hate crime. The

Guardian. https://www.theguardian.com/uk-news/2018/feb/22/white-powder-letter-prince-harry-meghan-markle-anthrax-scare

Ensor, J., Our Foreign Staff, Martin, D., Furness, H., Sabur, R., & Telegraph Sport. (2011, March 18). Prince William in pictures. Sunday Telegraph. https://www.telegraph.co.uk/news/picturegalleries/royalty/8371264/Prince-William-in-pictures.html

Evans, M., & Reslen, E. (2018, January 24). A definitive history of Prince Harry and Meghan Markle's royal relationship. Town & Country. https://www.townandcountrymag.com/society/a9664508/prince-harry-meghan-markle-relationship/

Evening Standard. (2012, December 4). Saturdays' Mollie King admits: "I did date Prince Harry." Evening Standard. https://www.standard.co.uk/showbiz/celebrity-news/saturdays-mollie-king-admits-i-did-date-prince-harry-8382007.html

Fritz, A. (2020, November 23). The comment Prince Charles made after harry's birth that broke Princess Diana's heart. Reader's Digest.

https://www.rd.com/article/comment-prince-charles-made-after-harrys-birth/

Gammell, C., Howse, C., Berry, S., Zeqiri, D., Telegraph Reporters, Maxted, A., & Tsang, S. (2008, February 28). How the Prince Harry blackout was broken. Sunday Telegraph. https://www.telegraph.co.uk/news/uknews/1580111/How-the-Prince-Harry-blackout-was-broken.html

Grierson, J. (2022, December 5). Prince Harry speaks of 'suffering' of women marrying into royal family. The Guardian. https://www.theguardian.com/uk-news/2022/dec/05/prince-harry-women-marrying-royal-family-meghan-netflix

Haynes, S. (Originally published: September 23, 2019). Prince Harry is honoring his mother's work in Angola. Here's what to know about Princess Diana's landmines walk. Time. https://time.com/5682006/princess-diana-landmines/

Head, G. W. H. (2017, January 17). Top ten redheads in literature and mythology. Girl with Her Head in a Book.

https://girlwithherheadinabook.co.uk/2017/01/top-ten-redheads-in-literature-and-mythology.html

Hicks, A. (2021, April 24). Pippa Middleton made cheeky joke after her bum sparked frenzy at Kate's wedding. Dailystar.co.uk. https://www.dailystar.co.uk/news/latest-news/how-pippa-middletons-bum-sparked-23882363

How Princess Diana changed attitudes to Aids. (2017, April 5). BBC. https://www.bbc.com/news/av/magazine-39490507

Howse, C., Arasteh, A., Telegraph Reporters, McGrath, M., & Telegraph Sport. (2008, February 28). Prince Harry in Taliban gun battle. Sunday Telegraph. https://www.telegraph.co.uk/news/uknews/1580113/Prince-Harry-in-Taliban-gun-battle.html

Hussein, A. (n.d.). Prince Charles, Prince of Wales and Diana, Princess of Wales, wearing. Getty Images. https://www.gettyimages.com/detail/news-photo/prince-charles-prince-of-wales-and-diana-princess-of-wales-news-photo/186528976

Independent. i.e., Newsdesk. (2018, June 19). Britain's Prince Harry and Meghan Markle set for first trip abroad as newlyweds with Dublin tour. Irish Independent. https://www.independent.ie/style/celebrity/celebrity-news/britains-prince-harry-and-meghan-markle-set-for-first-trip-abroad-as-newlyweds-with-dublin-tour-37026481.html

Kirkpatrick, E. (2020, December 14). Princess Eugenie and her husband have reportedly already moved out of harry and Meghan's Old House. Vanity Fair. https://www.vanityfair.com/style/2020/12/princess-eugenie-husband-frogmore-cottage-move-out-prince-harry-meghan-markle

Levenson, D. (n.d.). Prince Harry with headmistress Jane Mynors on his first day at. Getty Images. https://www.gettyimages.com/detail/news-photo/prince-harry-with-headmistress-jane-mynors-on-his-first-day-news-photo/1073701850

Lowe, L. (2022, December 8). Harry and Meghan first met on Instagram after he saw her with a dog-ears filter. TODAY. https://www.today.com/popculture/royals/harry-meghan-first-met-instagram-rcna60719

Lyons, K. (2018, October 19). Bearing a baby and banana bread, Harry and Meghan enchant Australia. The Guardian. https://www.theguardian.com/uk-news/2018/oct/19/prince-harry-meghan-australia-duke-duchess-sussex

Majendie, P. (2008, March 1). Prince Harry: Wild child turned war hero. Reuters. https://www.reuters.com/article/uk-britain-harry-image-idUSL2968319120080301

Mansoor, S., & Haynes, S. (Originally published: November 17, 2019). Prince Andrew says he doesn't regret his "very useful" relationship with Jeffrey Epstein. Time. https://time.com/5731244/prince-andrew-interview-epstein/

McTaggart, I., Rayner, G., Ward, V., Coen, S., Bond, J., Tominey, C., Sawer, P., & Hazell, W. (2022, September 17). Heart of oak - international spotlight on Queen Elizabeth's coffin. Sunday Telegraph. https://www.telegraph.co.uk/royal-family/2022/09/17/heart-oak-international-spotlight-queen-elizabeths-coffin/

Meghan Markle 'Suits' up for success [INTERVIEW]. (2016, February 29). EBONY Media Operations.

https://www.ebony.com/meghan-markle-suits-interview/

Our history. (n.d.). The HALO Trust. https://www.halotrust.org/about-us/who-we-are/our-history/

Page 5736. (n.d.). Thegazette.co.uk. https://www.thegazette.co.uk/London/issue/58667/supplement/5736

Pierce, A., Howse, C., Zeqiri, D., Arasteh, A., Telegraph Reporters, & McGrath, M. (2008, May 5). Prince Harry receives Afghan medal. Sunday Telegraph. https://www.telegraph.co.uk/news/uknews/theroyalfamily/1929243/Prince-Harry-receives-Afghan-medal.html

Royal Family to pay tribute to His Royal Highness Prince Philip Duke of Edinburgh in new BBC One film. (n.d.). BBC. https://web.archive.org/web/20210909113619/https://www.bbc.co.uk/mediacentre/2021/prince-philip-the-family-remembers

Sadat, H. (2017). Harry & Meghan: A Royal Engagement. Pitkin Publishing.

Scobie, O., & Webber, S. (2016, April 29). Prince Harry and his pregnant ex-girlfriend Natalie Pinkham attend the same event: See the photos. Us Weekly. https://www.usmagazine.com/celebrity-news/news/prince-harry-ex-girlfriend-natalie-pinkham-attend-same-event-w204568/

Sisavat, M. (2021, April 7). Prince Harry's Invictus Games finally have a new date — get all the details! POPSUGAR. https://www.popsugar.com/celebrity/where-will-prince-harry-invictus-games-be-held-in-2022-47110353

Smith, A. (2022, September 12). Meghan Markle's best speeches — from the UN Women Conference to One Young World. Evening Standard. https://www.standard.co.uk/insider/meghan-markle-best-speeches-solo-royal-invictus-games-one-young-world-b1023598.html

Stump, S. (2013, August 12). Prince Harry continues Diana's charity work in Africa. TODAY. https://www.today.com/news/prince-harry-continues-dianas-charity-work-africa-6C10897069

Taylor, A. (2021, March 11). Harry and Meghan: What's the media's "invisible contract" with British royalty? BBC. https://www.bbc.com/news/entertainment-arts-56326807

The. (1986, April 13). The early education of a future king. The New York Times. https://www.nytimes.com/1986/04/13/education/the-early-education-of-a-future-king.html

The official website of The Duke & Duchess of Sussex. (n.d.). The Official Website of The Duke & Duchess of Sussex. Retrieved December 9, 2022, from https://sussexroyal.com/

Tyler perry's Atlanta mansion sells to Steve Harvey & sets another record! (2020, June 8). Top Ten Real Estate Deals. https://toptenrealestatedeals.com/weekly-ten-best-home-deals/home/tyler-perrys-atlanta-mansion-sells-to-steve-harvey-sets-another-record

Waterson, J. (2018, May 20). Royal wedding confirmed as year's biggest UK TV event. The Guardian. https://www.theguardian.com/uk-news/2018/may/20/royal-wedding-confirmed-as-years-biggest-uk-tv-event

When princes Harry and William visited Canada with their parents. (Last Updated: October 18, 2021). CBC News. https://www.cbc.ca/archives/charles-diana-william-harry-visit-canada-ontario-1991-1.5316289

Wong, C. M. (2022, September 22). Tyler Perry shares what he learned by offering home to prince harry and Meghan Markle. HuffPost. https://www.huffpost.com/entry/tyler-perry-meghan-markle-prince-harry_n_632ca384e4b087fae6fdd9c0

(N.d.-a). Archive.org. https://web.archive.org/web/20090202113324/http://www.princeofwales.gov.uk/personalprofiles/theprinceofwales/atwork/supportingthequeen/countriesvisited/index.html

(N.d.-b). Com.au. https://www.news.com.au/lifestyle/real-life/true-stories/the-infamous-taped-phone-call-behind-squidgygate/news-story/74a4c6f27899e2b6317cf7e4866844ab

(N.d.-c). Archive.org. https://web.archive.org/web/20120617111409/http://www.13wham.com/media/lib/16/3/2/b/32bae36e-

1ae2-4047-b24c-070c87068271/ERIC_SMITH___2012.pdf

(N.d.-d). Archive.org.
https://web.archive.org/web/20080304115059/http://au.lifestyle.yahoo.com/b/new-idea/8771/prince-harry-goes-to-war-in-afghanistan

Printed in Great Britain
by Amazon